CHESS FOR BEGINNERS

A Complete Overview of the Board,
Pieces, Rules, and Strategies to Win

By: Game Nest

ISBN: 978-1-951791-39-1

Get All Our New Releases For FREE!

Sign up to our VIP Newsletter to get all of our future releases absolutely free!

www.gamenest.org/free

Table of Contents

Chapter 1: An Introduction to Chess

What is Chess?

To begin with, it is a game. It can be played for fun, competition, personal mastery, or profit. Generally, it's a zero-sum game, meaning in every game, the winner's victory is equal to the loser's defeat. It is also a game of skill, meaning a player's chances of victory are improved by proper implementation of strategy and tactics. In fact, the unintended depth behind this seemingly simple game has made it the obsession of countless game masters throughout its history. Today, chess is one of the most enduring, popular, and well-studied games in the world.

If you're reading this guide, you've probably been drawn to the game just like the rest of us. That's understandable—chess is a pastime that can be as deep or shallow as you want. You could end up devoting as little time as a game or two a week, or become an avid player engaging in multiple games per day. A few end up committing most of their lives to the game, but however much you put into chess, you'll always get a return on your investment.

What is it that makes chess so appealing to so many people? The answer may vary depending on who you ask. Some find it to be a calming hobby, a chance to shut out the noise of the outside world and lose oneself in the infinite depth of the game. For others, it's a breakneck competitive outlet and an opportunity to feel the rush of personal improvement. No matter who you are or why you play, however, understanding the fundamentals of the game is a sure way to enhance your experience. Just as in any kind of art, sport, or craft, a trained eye is capable of interpreting and enjoying more details in every aspect of the hobby.

That's where *A Chess Beginner's Guide* comes in. With this book in hand, you will be gaining a valuable head-start into understanding the many intricacies of chess. As you read on from the game's storied history to its evolving modern strategies, you'll come to fully understand why this game of 32 pieces and 64 squares continues to fascinate people and cultures all over the world.

History of the Game

The precise origins of chess remain a mystery, with historians and anthropologists still debating over the subject. What's generally agreed, however, is that the earliest known ancestor of the game originated in India sometime before the 6th century CE. This early predecessor, called *chaturanga*, was quite different from the game we know today. A war game, *chaturanga* took its name from a military formation mentioned in the epic *Mahabharata*. The formation itself refers to four divisions within the army: infantry, cavalry, chariotry, and elephantry.

As *chaturanga* evolved, so did the names it was known by. Around 600 CE, *chatrang* became a growing pastime in Persia and Central Asia where it later spread to further east, gaining recognition with different cultures, calling it different names. In Mongolia, it was called *shatar*, in China, *xiangqi*, and in Japan, *shogi*. Each culture brought its unique perspective to the rules of the game and the character of the pieces, but two fundamental qualities of *chaturanga* persisted in each variation. First, unlike in checkers, different pieces had different capabilities. Second, capturing the opponent's king was the path to victory. These qualities remain fundamental to the DNA of modern chess.

Chess reached Europe by the 10th century CE by way of expanding the Islamic Empire. When *chatrang* was introduced to the Arab world, it was redubbed *shatranj* but remained largely similar to the Persian variation of the game.

The early Islamic conquests brought bloodshed to both the Levant and the Iberian Peninsula but also brought cultural and technological innovations, including *shatranj*. The Greeks called it *zatrikion*, while in Spain, it became known as *ajedrez*. Both cultures initially retained the Persian names given to each piece. As the game spread throughout the medieval world, the Persian word *shāh* ("king") gradually evolved into the English *chess*. The phrase *"Shāh Māt!"* ("the king is helpless") would likewise develop into the modern term *checkmate*.

Chess quickly took the European world by storm as it became so popular that at times both the church and secular authorities attempted to prohibit the games—and the gambling that often came with it. Eventually, the names of the pieces began to change to reflect the local culture. Elephants became bishops and the *vazīr*, or minister, became the queen.

The rules of the game continued to change as well. By 1300, an addition had been made to the rules, allowing pawns to move two squares on their first move. Later, sometime before 1500, the previously weak queen and bishops gained new abilities to make them more useful and to speed up play. This modified ruleset, once referred to as Queen's Chess, developed into the modern standard of play by the 19th century.

Since the birth of modern competitive chess in 1851, when German-born Adolf Anderssen won the first-ever international chess tournament, the sport has exploded into a worldwide phenomenon. Countless grandmasters, men, and women hailing from dozens of countries around the world have risen to prominence throughout the decades.

In the late 20th Century, chess even became a topic of a heated political conversation. When the 1972 World Chess Championship pitted American prodigy Bobby Fischer against Russian champion Boris Spassky, both of the rival nations took immense interest in the match's outcome. When Fischer won the match, ending 24 years of Soviet dominance in competitive play, it was touted as a blow against the USSR itself. Later, when Fischer defied U.S. sanctions to attend an unofficial rematch against Spassky in 1992, a warrant was issued for his arrest.

Today, the *Fédération Internationale des Échecs* (FIDE) acts as the governing body of competitive chess worldwide. New names have come to prominence in recent years, including Hungary's Judit Polgar, widely considered as the strongest female player in the history of the game. The current reigning champion, Magnus Carlsen of Norway, holds the highest peak classical rating in history with a score of 2882.

Using This Guide

The purpose of this book is to introduce new players to the game: its mechanics, strategies, and the joys of playing. It's meant for both brand-new players and those with some knowledge who are looking to deepen their understanding.

We recommend that you read each section sequentially from start to finish. While all terms are outlined when they first appear, you can circle back to the glossary at the end of this book for a quick refresher. Otherwise, the book makes the most sense when each chapter is read in order.

You've already read *Chapter 1: An Introduction to Chess*. In *Chapter 2: The Board and Pieces*, you'll familiarize yourself with how to read algebraic chess notation and learn how to read diagrams. You'll also learn the movement options for each piece, as well as a brief overview of the common strategic uses of each piece. Finally, you'll receive an overview of standard piece values as determined by a majority of strategists.

With this knowledge in hand, you will then progress to *Chapter 3: Beginner Strategies*. While Chapter 2 deals predominantly in concrete terms with specific in-game meanings, this section appeals more to the abstract thinker. Chapter 3 introduces several high-level strategic concepts and is divided into three sections covering the main phases of chess: opening, middlegame, and endgame. .

Finally, in *Chapter 4: How to Start Playing Chess*, you're going to learn well, just that! In addition to advice on how to find a good local chess club or get started playing online, the closing section of this guide provides further study tools as you grow into a more advanced player. From reading lists to databases, there's an endless, ever-growing selection of chess knowledge out there, just waiting to be studied.

So, let's get started. Today, you will be taking what may as well be your very first steps as a chess player. Someday, with dedication and continuous study, you might find yourself writing the next great book on chess! It's your path to pave, and whether you're just looking for a fun new hobby or already have your sights set on grandmaster status, this guide is here to help.

Chapter 2: The Board and Pieces

Section 1 – The Board

To understand the roles of the various pieces used in a game of chess, one must first understand how to navigate the board itself. Traditionally, chess is played on a grid composed of eight rows and eight columns, referred to as *ranks* and *files*, respectively. Tiles on the grid alternate between two colors. While the colors used on individual boards vary, the lighter color is typically referred to as *White*, while the darker color is usually *Black*.

With 64 total tiles and countless possible ways for each game to play out, describing specific positions on the board is essential to strategic discourse. As early as the 17th century, early modes of chess notation had begun to develop, providing ways to describe both the board and the positions of pieces. Up until recently, various forms of descriptive notation were used by strategists writing in English. Today, the algebraic notation is used internationally.

While it can be intimidating at first, the algebraic notation is one of the smoothest ways to discuss and understand chess strategy. The principles are basic: each rank is numbered 1-8, and each file is assigned a lowercase letter from a-h.

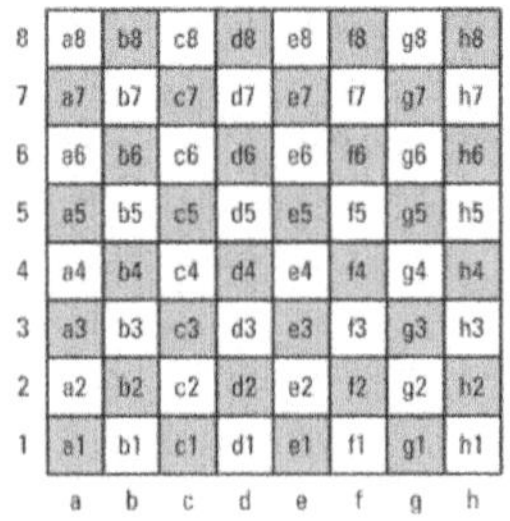

Figure 1: A blank chessboard with algebraic notation labeling the files and ranks. In algebraic notation, White is assumed to start play with pieces on the "bottom" of the

board at ranks 1 and 2 while Black starts with pieces on the "top" of the board at ranks 7 and 8.

These letters and numbers work together to describe each tile on the board. For example, in algebraic notation, the lower-left corner of the board would be called a1, the upper right corner h8. The square four rows right and three up would be d3.

Now that you've begun to understand the board through algebraic notation, adding pieces to it should be much simpler. Each piece has a corresponding uppercase letter. Alternatively, pieces can be notated with their corresponding figurines. Examples of each are shown below.

Chess Piece	Letter	Figurine
King	K	♔ ♚
Queen	Q	♕ ♛
Rook	R	♖ ♜
Bishop	B	♗ ♝
Knight	N	♘ ♞
Pawn	P	♙ ♟

Remember, uppercase letters refer to pieces. Lowercase letters refer to the files on the board. So, while B refers to a piece, the bishop, b refers to the second file from the left.

When a piece moves, we write it out in algebraic notation by listing the uppercase letter first, indicating the piece, followed by the file that the piece has moved to, and finally, the rank to which it moved. A rook moving to f4 would thus be written out as Rf4. The only exception to this is the movement for pawns. While a pawn can be signified with an uppercase P, it can also be indicated by a lack of uppercase letters. For example, if you're reading a record of piece movements and you see e5, you can assume that it means that a pawn moved into that square.

Figure 2: In this diagram, we would notate the white bishop's movement as Bd3

If two or more of the same type of piece could have moved to the same square on the same turn, we use notation to disambiguate by including the file and rank of the square from which the piece was moved for the sake of clarity. This added notation comes after the uppercase letter of the moving piece, but before the coordinates that piece moved to. If two rooks on the same rank could both have moved to d4, writing Rbd4 indicates that the rook that moved there started from file b. If instead, the two rooks were on the same rank, we might write it as R2d4.

When one piece captures another, it's indicated in notation using a lowercase x. Nxe3 would indicate a Knight moving to capture a piece on e3. If the movement of a piece puts the opposing king in check, a + sign is indicated at the end of the notation. If that same knight's movement had put the opposing king in check, we'd write it as Nxe3+. Similarly, the end of a game is signified by a # sign at the end of the notation, representing a checkmate.

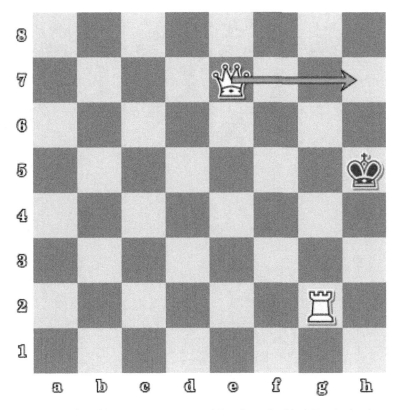

Figure 3: Here, the white queen can move to h7 and put the black king in checkmate. This would be written as Qh7#

This is all there is to it. While there are a few other special cases that will be covered later in this section, these are the basic symbols you'll need to understand most concerning chess notation. All that's left is learning to put it all together.

A full game of chess is written out in notation by listing every move in sequential order. Each move consists of White and Black taking their respective turns. In notation, White's turn is always written first, followed by Black's turn. The move itself is indicated by its number.

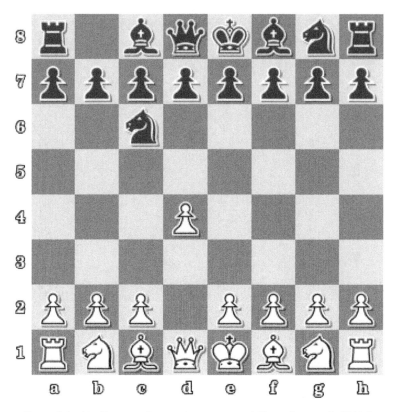

Figure 4: In this diagram, the opening move would be written as 1. d4 Nc6

Additional moves are listed until one player achieves checkmate and the game is over. The results of the game are written out as 1-0 if White won, 0-1 if Black won.

If you're feeling confident in your understanding of chess notation at this point, that's excellent. If it hasn't stuck yet, don't worry. You don't need to understand notation to play and enjoy chess, but it does help if you're studying strategy or reviewing an old game. For the casual player, all you really need to understand is that while 64 squares may not seem much to keep track of, the possibilities you can unlock on each one of them are nearly countless.

In the next several sections, we will discuss the unique abilities of each piece, how games are decided, and the various beginner strategies you can employ throughout each phase of the game. If you start feeling overwhelmed at any point, you can always return to this section for a quick refresher on the meanings of various symbols in algebraic notation.

Section 2 – The Pawn

A stalwart formation of soldiers—weak individually, but strong when they stand together—prepares to intercept an enemy assault. A single intrepid foot-soldier races across the battlefield, evading incoming attacks with the hope that his experience will make him stronger. A pack of warriors sits waiting to spring their ambush, knowing that they've been overlooked by their unsuspecting foes.

The pawn embodies all these concepts in a single piece. Originally representing the infantry of an army, pawns were once considered the least valuable pieces on the game. As chess evolved into the modern game we play today; however, rules were added to make the pawn a more dynamic piece. In modern chess, proper deployment of pawns can be the difference between winning and losing a game.

Filling the front ranks of each color's army, both players begin the game with eight pawns. This makes them the most numerous pieces on the board, though they're often the first to be eliminated in early exchanges.

Movement for Pawns

Throughout a game, a pawn generally has three movement options available to it. At any point, a pawn can move a single space forward, provided that space is not blocked by another piece. If a pawn has not yet moved in a game, that pawn can instead move two spaces forward, provided neither space ahead of it is blocked.

If a pawn can't move into a space occupied by another piece, how is it meant to battle enemies? Pawns are unique among pieces in that they possess a special movement option only available when they capture an enemy. A pawn can capture any unit by moving diagonally forward into that piece's space. The pawn captures in what may be called the V way of capture, where it captures the piece of the enemy that is diagonal to it, either on the right or on the left, thereby occupying that square. An example is shown below.

Figure 5: In this scenario, the pawn on d4 can capture the enemy on e5. Doing so would leave it vulnerable to capture by the enemy pawn on d6, however.

In rare cases, a pawn may use a fourth movement option to capture. This option is called *en passant* (French for "in passing"), and it requires a variety of conditions be met before it can be used.

1. The capturing pawn must be on its fifth rank
2. The pawn being captured must have moved forward two squares from its starting square on the previous turn
3. The capture must take place on the turn immediately after the captured pawn moved
4. The pawn being captured must be on a file adjacent to the capturing pawn

If all four of these conditions aren't met, then an *en passant* capture isn't legal. For example, if all four conditions are met, but the player chooses to move a different piece on that turn, they cannot initiate the *en passant* capture on their next turn. The opportunity has slipped through their grasp!

When an *en passant* capture does occur, the capturing pawn doesn't move into the space of the captured pawn. Instead, it moves diagonally into the captured pawn's file, but one space forward: the capturing pawn occupies the square in which the captured pawn had skipped while making the two squares move from its starting point. It's unique in being the only type of capture in which the capturing piece moves to a different space than the captured piece.

In algebraic notation, an *en passant* capture is indicated by the letter e.p. at the end of a move.

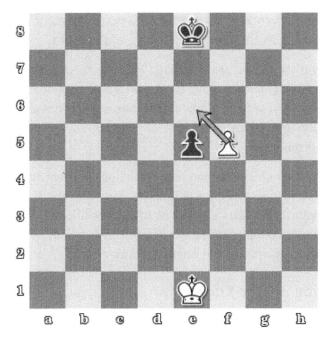

Figure 6: Assuming the black pawn has just moved forward two spaces, the conditions for an en passant *capture have all been met. The white pawn may move diagonally to e6 and remove the black pawn from the board. This move would be notated as fxe6e.p.*

The rules for pawn movement may seem convoluted, but remember that no matter the type of movement they're using, pawns can only move forward on the board. A pawn can neither move nor capture backward. In fact, they even gain a special reward for making it all the way to the opposite side.

Pawn Promotion

When a pawn of either color makes it to the opposite end of the board, that pawn can immediately be promoted to a different piece of the same color. The promoted pawn can be replaced with a knight, bishop, rook, or even an additional queen. The only piece it can't promote to is a king.

Adding another queen to the mix can quickly turn an endgame scenario on its head, and skilled players may even have a pawn promoted in the middlegame. To prevent an opponent from gaining this tremendous advantage, most players always take steps to ensure enemy pawns don't draw too close to their edge of the board.

To keep the pawns protected and increase their odds of promotion, players should generally move their pawns along the board in groups of two or more. These formations, sometimes called connected pawns, can defend one another as they block off enemy movements and journey towards promotion.

Due to their versatility and unique abilities, a pawn should never be underestimated. As you grow as a player and strategist, keep a close eye on how your opponents use pawns to gain positional advantages. You may be able to adopt their tactics as your own, or may even be inspired to utilize your pawns in your original strategy.

Section 3 – The Knight

While infantry formations clash, a rider on horseback effortlessly maneuvers around the stalemate, flanking her enemies and creating a vital opening. As their shape suggests, the knights of a chess game symbolize an army's cavalry units. Although their unique movement pattern makes them slow to travel the board, it also makes them capable of feats no other piece can perform.

Movement for Knights

Mastering the knight can be challenging, even for experienced players. Unlike any other piece, the knight moves either two spaces vertically and one horizontally, or one space vertically and two horizontally. In either case, the movement takes on an "L" shape.

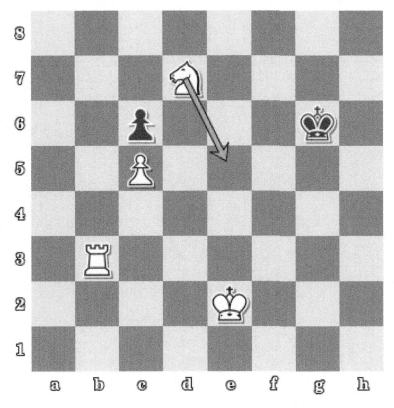

Figure 7: Black's king is in trouble! With its "L" shaped movement, White's knight can move to e5 this turn, putting the enemy king in check.

While a knight can only move three squares at a time, it's also the only piece that can move over squares occupied by other pieces. Whether these pieces are allies or enemies, the knight simply "jumps" over them to reach its destination. It only captures a piece if it ends its movement on that piece's square.

Center of the Action

With its unique method of maneuverability, knights make excellent controllers of the board, especially in the early game, when pieces are tightly grouped. To maximize their value, players will generally want to position their knights near the middle of the board, where they can attack the most squares.

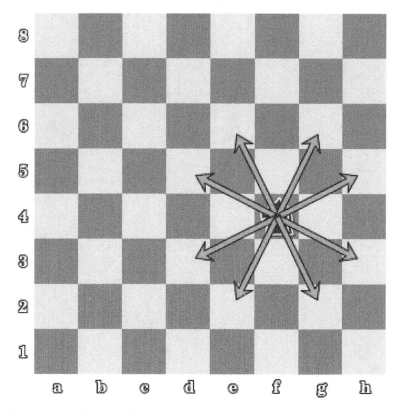

Figure 8: From this desirable position near the center of the board, Black's knight can capture on eight different positions with its movement. A knight positioned this way is sometimes referred to as an octopus!

Many opening strategies rely on the knight's ability to overcome the walls of enemy pawns and halt early advances. Knights lose some of their value as the game progresses, as they're less useful for cornering a king and achieving a checkmate. Still, they provide an important material asset at any point in the game. A wise player can leverage their knights throughout the game, sacrificing them at a key moment to allow other pieces to maneuver, or deliver the final death knell to a penned-in king.

Section 4 – The Bishop

A loping elephant towering over the battlefield, a keen huntsman striking from a great distance, or an influential abbot exercising his authority—the bishop has undergone significant changes across various cultures. No matter what name you might know it by, this piece excels on an open board, where it can extend its full and frightening reach.

Just like the knight, bishops are generally considered pieces of middling value. But while knights prefer the crowded board of a game's opening, a bishop's true strength shines in the middle and endgames.

Movement for Bishops

Like a capturing pawn, the bishops move diagonally along the board and capture any enemy whose space they move into. Unlike the pawn, however, a bishop's range is limited only by the pieces standing in its way. As a result of this, the relative strength of a bishop is greatly influenced by how much freedom it has on the board. For example, a bishop penned in by its own pawns is colloquially called a "bad bishop."

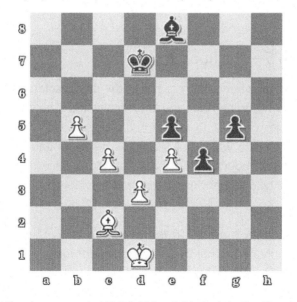

Figure 9: In the above scenario, White's bishop is blockade by its allies, preventing it from threatening the enemy king. Black's bishop has no such disadvantage and is well-positioned for an attack.

17

Since bishops move diagonally, a bishop that begins play on a white square will only ever occupy a white square, while a bishop starting on a black square will only ever occupy black squares. Each player begins with one bishop of each type and should keep this in mind when maneuvering other pieces. Leaving paths open to your bishops is a key part of using them strategically, especially if you wish to develop them early in the game.

Far-reaching Hands

While often impeded in the opening game by large clusters of pieces, a studious player can exercise the bishop's speed and reach early on to put significant pressure on their opponent. A well-hidden, well-positioned bishop can pose a serious threat to the opponent's undeveloped back ranks, potentially with little risk to itself.

However, it's in the middle and late game, that most players begin mobilizing their bishops earnestly. A bishop's control of the board only grows as more space becomes available for them to maneuver, and unlike a pair of knights, two bishops are enough to trap a king in checkmate.

Section 5 – The Rook

A thunder of wheels clatters across the dirt as soldiers clear a path—the chariotry has joined the fray, and they will not be slowed. Watching as his enemies close in around him, a prudent king retreats within the safety of his castle walls, bolstering his defenses and giving himself a superior vantage point. The rook is a dangerous piece in the hands of any player, but a true student of the game knows how to maximize its many advantages.

Considered second only to the queen in terms of power, rooks are hampered only by their slow route to development in the early game. Additionally, cunning players may try to target an opponent's rooks before they've even had a chance to deploy them. To protect these precious pieces, one must understand how to use them effectively.

Movement for Rooks

Similar to the bishop, a rook has no limit on its range. It can move anywhere in a turn, provided it has a clear path. Rooks, however, enjoy the benefit of moving orthogonally, rather than diagonally. That is, they move in straight lines either horizontally or vertically.

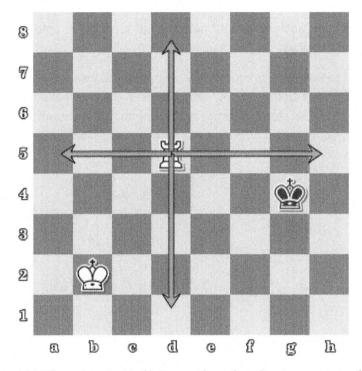

Figure 10: With no pieces to stand in its way, the rook on d5 can move to any of the squares on the same file or rank.

This makes rooks incredibly useful for boxing in enemies and holding down defensive lines. They also possess a significant offensive capability, especially as space becomes available for them to maneuver. A pair of uncontested rooks can quickly spell the end for an enemy king. Although their high power and simple movement pattern mean that some players utilize them as blunt instruments, a skilled tactician never underestimates the complexity a rook can bring to the game. Due to their offensive capabilities, some also refer to them as boundary setters because of the vast range they could cover.

Tactical Retreat

One of the few glaring weaknesses of the rook is that they begin the game from the corners of the board. Since they lack diagonal movement or the ability to jump over pieces, it can be difficult to deploy them until at least a few pawns are cleared away. A player who fails to develop their rooks for too long may find out that these powerful pieces fall prey to weaker units such as the bishops or knights, rendered helpless by their surrounding allies.

The rooks have a unique ability to combat this weakness that can only be performed under special circumstances. When a rook that has not moved from its starting corner and a king that has not moved from his starting square, with no pieces standing between them, those two pieces can take on a special movement called *castling*.

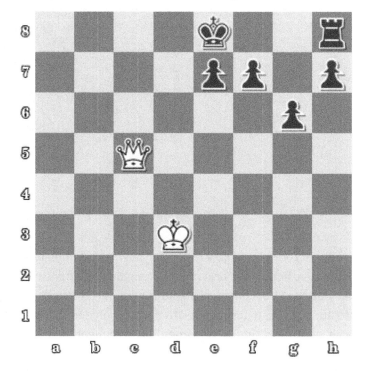

Figure 11: Assuming neither piece has moved yet in this game, Black's king and rook may castle on this turn. In this case, the king would move to g8, and the rook would move to f8.

Additional conditions for castling are that the king cannot castle if it is currently in check, would end the move in check, or would move through any space that would put it in check. The castling rook does not face this restriction.

Castling can be done with either rook as long as all conditions are met. In either case, the king moves two spaces towards the starting position of the rook it's castling with, then the rook occupies the square the king skipped when making the two spaces move. If the castling rook is on file h or *kingside*, it moves to file f. If the rook starts on file a, or *queenside*, it moves to file d. This is the only means by which a player might move two pieces in a single turn, and the only movement other than a knight's which allows pieces to "jump" over one another. In algebraic notation, kingside castling is written as 0-0, while queenside castling is written as 0-0-0.

With its blend of sheer power and strategic versatility, the rook is a highly valuable piece in most chess strategies. While they often wait until the endgame to show their full potential, most players will attempt to develop their rooks sooner than later. In fact, there is only one piece in the game that can outclass the rook in terms of power and value.

Section 6 – The Queen

Surveying the clashing military formations spread across the field before her, the queen prepares to put her master plan into action. Though she may not wield the same authority as her king, only a fool would take her lightly. She is always watching, waiting, and nothing is beyond her reach.

The queen is widely regarded as the most powerful piece in any chess game; some players even tend to resign after losing their queen. Thanks to its extreme maneuverability, the queen is a dominating presence at nearly any point in the game. Like any other piece, however, one mistake is all it takes for it to fall into enemy clutches. There's no one correct way to utilize your queen, but understanding her full potential will help you determine for yourself whether you'd prefer to use it more aggressively or conservatively.

Movement for the Queen

The queen's movement is the combination of the movement options of the bishop and rook: diagonally, horizontally, and vertically. While it lacks the knight's ability to move through occupied squares, her variety of options makes it extremely difficult to box the queen in. This also makes it a devastating offensive unit, capable of developing quickly through multiple openings on the board.

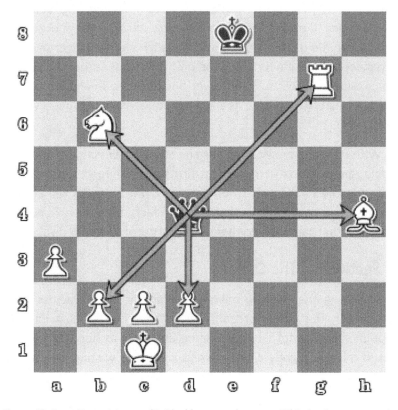

Figure 12: From its position on d4, Black's queen threatens White's pieces across the board.

Risk and Reward

Due to its remarkable versatility, the queen is a staple of any successful strategy. Even a single queen can wreak havoc on enemy ranks. However, an overextended queen can be easily picked off without other pieces supporting it. Even a guarded queen is far from invulnerable, as many players are willing to sacrifice a lesser piece to remove their enemy's greatest weapon.

Beginning players—and even experienced ones—will often struggle to find the right balance of offense and defense when it comes time to deploy their queen. While all-out aggression can secure an early material advantage, players who rely too much on the strength of their queen are often easily picked apart when the keystone of their strategy is ripped away. Conversely, an overly cautious player too afraid to lose his/her queen may never have the chance to take advantage of her power.

Ultimately, each player must find the balance that's best suited to their playing style, but neither extreme is recommended. In general, every piece should be treated as a valuable resource, but not even the queen is irreplaceable. The only piece that's required to win is the king, and there may come a time where you must sacrifice your queen to gain a critical advantage.

Section 7 – The King

Knights and bishops alike rally under his banner. Battles are won and lost on the strength of his wits. While he may not possess the raw prowess of a trained soldier, a wise commander knows better than to assume that the king is ever defenseless. After all, the king is the foundation on which the army stands, and there's no sacrifice his soldiers won't make to protect him.

The king is something of a paradox—simultaneously one of the weakest pieces as well as the most valuable. For this reason, the king is usually played defensively, but a skilled tactician might surprise an opponent with an unexpected flurry of offense. In this section, you'll learn the basics of keeping your king protected, as well as how to turn it from a liability into an asset.

Movement for the King

The king's movement is the simplest of any piece: it can move one square in any direction. This makes it only slightly more maneuverable than the pawn. As it lacks the possibility of promotion, one could argue that the king is the least versatile piece on the board. Despite this, failing to protect your king means certain defeat. Once the king is cornered, that's checkmate—Game over.

It might seem counterintuitive for the most important piece in the game to be the weakest, but the nature of chess necessitates this. If the king had better movement options, games could take significantly longer. In fact, some earlier rulesets provided the king with more versatile movement, such as the option to move like a knight once per game. The result was games that usually ended only after a long, drawn-out struggle, usually requiring most or all of the other pieces to be cleared from the board. Thus, the king's power remains limited.

Wielding Authority

For most beginners, the king should be used primarily in a defensive capacity. However, this doesn't mean you should simply wait for enemies to come to you. As early as your first few moves, you can begin positioning your king to make it harder for your opponent to threaten him. Techniques like castling can provide an early advantage and increase your chances of survival as well as an opportunity to advance.

As you grow in experience and become more comfortable with the game, you can start exploring ways to turn your king into a credible threat. In the middle and late games, the king can fill valuable gaps in your formation, or lure unwary attackers into a trap.

Section 8 – Piece Valuations

Based on the power and usefulness of each of the pieces listed above, various strategists have attempted to assign relative values to each piece throughout the history of chess. While these value systems can never fully capture the complexity of the game, they're helpful as a kind of shorthand for both new and experienced players. In modern play, the following piece values are most commonly accepted.

Piece	♟ Pawn	♞ Knight	♝ Bishop	♜ Rook	♛ Queen
Value	1	3	3	5	9

At the lowest end, we see the pawn, who must rely on their large numbers and ability to support one another to overcome their individual weaknesses. Of course, a pawn can eventually promote to a queen, so you don't want to simply throw them away.

Next comes the knights and bishops, tied with a relative value of 3. Rooks are considered to be slightly stronger, while the queen holds a whopping 9 of 9. As you can see, the king is the only piece not listed with a standard value because it can't be lost or traded. Effectively, the king is invaluable.

Of course, the practical value of these pieces can vary significantly throughout the game. Factors such as piece synergy and the makeup of the board go a long way in determining how much use an individual piece will provide. To better account for this, some systems attempt to use various value combinations of pieces or even pieces at different stages of the game

Variable Values

In general, pawns tend to increase their value the closer they draw to promotion. For instance, a pawn on the 6th rank has far greater value than an undeveloped pawn. However, this isn't the only factor influencing a pawn's worth. A *passed pawn* or a pawn with no opposing pawns on the same or adjacent files is considered particularly valuable because of its ability to move freely across the board. Likewise, *connected pawns* on adjacent files can defend each other and are considered preferable to an isolated pawn.

Figure 13: The pawns on c5 and d4 are both connected and passed. Little stands in their way on the path to promotion, unlike the opposing pawns on file f.

While individual bishops and knights have the same value, different combinations of these pieces have different relative uses. Since either bishop in a pair controls a different color of the square, two bishops together can functionally control the entire board. This makes them slightly more desirable than a pair of knights, or even a knight and a bishop pair. Of course, if one or both of your bishops are unable to maneuver, their relative value is less.

The rooks and queens maintain relatively consistent values throughout the game, except that the rooks become slightly more valuable in the endgame. While the king has no specific value, it generally also becomes better at defending his allies later in the game.

Differences in Opinion

Most authorities agree on the 1-3-3-5-9 method of assigning relative value, but many alternatives have been presented over the years. While one could dedicate an entire book to the subject, we'll discuss just a few of the discrepancies and how they relate to the broader game.

One of the most common changes seen on the standard formula is that of making bishops slightly more important than the knights since paired bishops are slightly stronger. The specific values vary widely, of course. Many alternative systems propose that both knights and bishops should be valued slightly higher.

Another frequent disagreement is how, if at all, the king should be valued. When piece values are being used to program a computer, the king must have a value that properly communicates its importance in the game. For this reason, many computer programs have the king listed under arbitrarily massive values, but this isn't practical for human use.

When strategists do opt to assign a value to the king, it's generally on par with the minor pieces, possibly slightly stronger or weaker. While lacking the speed of a knight or bishop, a king's omnidirectional movement makes it particularly useful for defending clusters of pieces.

Uses for Relative Values

In addition to the modern use of informing today's chess-playing computer programs, valuation systems serve two major roles for players. First, they help developing players begin to understand which trades are advantageous and which are strategic traps. For example, a new player might not see a problem with sacrificing a rook to capture an opponent's bishop, even though this is generally an unfavorable trade.

The second major benefit is that the piece values provide a way to track the general state of play throughout a game. While positional advantages are important, they're also extremely difficult to quantify. By assigning value to each piece, we can effectively "keep score" throughout a game.

Of course, chess is a game that's won with a single decisive move, and not by accruing the most points. Furthermore, while sacrificing a piece of greater value for a lesser piece is usually a mistake, there are occasions where it provides a critical positional advantage. The exploitation of these holes in the valuation system is often the key to outmaneuvering computer programs.

While understanding the importance of the relative values of each piece as you play, you will begin to feel which pieces are the most integral to your unique strategy. Most experienced players rely on a balance of their own experience and the wisdom of piece values derived from the extensive player and computer data.

Chapter Overview

By reading this chapter, you've gained all the basic information you need to begin engaging critically with chess strategies. It can be difficult to understand algebraic notation, but as you encounter it more often, the letters and numbers will begin to connect more quickly with their relative positions on the board. With just a little practice, you'll be able to use algebraic notation as a convenient shorthand for discussing positions and movement in chess.

Speaking of movement, you should also have a grasp on the various methods by which each piece maneuvers around the board, including special movements like castling and *en passant*. One of the defining qualities of chess that gives it such complexity is the fact that each piece type has its unique movement. This can be hard to keep track of at first, but you don't need to worry. The more familiar you become with each piece and its peculiarities, the better you'll understand their various strategic uses, as well as their relative values.

If you need a refresher on algebraic notation or to get clarification on a piece's movement in subsequent chapters, simply flip back to the relevant section. With so much information, it might take a little while for everything to stick. This is normal, and even the greatest chess players regularly review these basics to ensure they stay sharp.

As you continue reading, you'll learn more about the three basic phases of a game: the opening, middlegame, and endgame. Keep in mind the various strengths and weaknesses of each piece as you study the strategies for each phase of the game. Anyone can follow the lines of an opening strategy—some are plotted out well beyond 30 moves! Being a genuinely talented player, however, means understanding why and how these strategies work. It all comes down to knowing your pieces.

Chapter 3: Beginner Strategies

Section 1 – Checkmate

In chess, success is determined by victory, and victory is determined by checkmate.

Checkmate occurs when a player's king is under threat of capture from one or more enemy pieces and cannot make a legal move to a safe square. When this happens, the player whose king is trapped loses, and their opponent is declared the winner.

It may seem strange to begin this chapter with the event that ends the game, but all of the chess strategies ultimately flow from the goal of checkmating your opponent and avoiding checkmate yourself. Every movement, offensive, and sacrifice must be made with the same ultimate purpose in mind. To that end, understanding the conditions of victory is essential to understanding all chess strategies, from the opening move to the final moments of the endgame.

Win, Lose, or Draw

While checkmate itself is a static target, there are as many paths to reach it as there are chess players. Some seek to place constant pressure directly on the enemy king, forcing the opponent to stay on the defensive until they make a fatal error. Others play the long game, picking off enemy pieces until the king is defenseless, or gaining minor positional advantages until their unsuspecting enemy is utterly trapped. Every strategy has its own advantages and complications that arise throughout various stages of play. It's up to you to determine which method is most appealing to your playstyle.

Aggressive players will derive great joy from regularly imposing *check*—the condition under which a king is threatened but can escape by moving away or blocking with another piece. An opponent forced into check has no choice but to respond defensively, making it difficult for them to mount a counterattack. However, this strategy carries a high risk: placing too much focus on an opponent's king may leave you vulnerable to an unforeseen ambush.

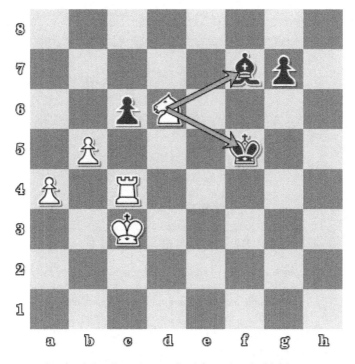

Figure 14: With White's knight imposing check from d6, Black's king must move to a safe location, potentially sacrificing the bishop on f7 in the process. Check can be one of the most effective ways of forcing an opponent to make an unfavorable trade.

More patient players may prefer to slowly reduce an opponent's forces while pursuing a long-term positional advantage. While this strategy generally runs a lower risk in the early and middle games, the longer the game drags on, the more opportunities your opponent may have to force a *stalemate*.

Stalemate occurs when the player whose turn is to play is not in check and has no legal moves available. When a stalemate occurs, the match immediately ends in a draw. This can be especially frustrating if you've spent dozens of moves with an upper hand, only to have your victory swept away and replaced with a draw.

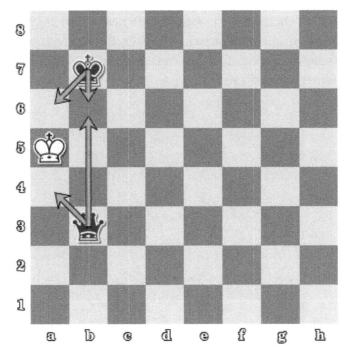

Figure 15: Black may seem to hold an advantage here, but they've let victory slip through their grasp by allowing White to draw in a stalemate since White has no moves available that would not put their king into check.

Apart from a stalemate, draws in chess are exceedingly rare, but not impossible. Conditions under which a draw can occur include the rule of *threefold repetition*, where the same board position has occurred three consecutive times from a particular player in a single match. The *fifty-move rule* is also a condition, in which each player makes 50 moves (total of 100) without a capture or pawn movement, or when a situation arises where checkmate is impossible for either player. Additionally, either player may offer a draw to their opponent at any time during a game. Such an offer can be accepted or declined at the other player's discretion.

Strategy 1: Fool's Mate

Now that you've obtained a thorough understanding of how chess is won and lost, we're ready to dive into the first of several beginner's strategies contained within this book. To begin, let's get acquainted with the fastest possible method of winning a chess game—referred to as *mate in two* or *Fool's Mate*.

While Fool's Mate requires a highly specific set of circumstances and isn't a particularly reliable route to victory, it does illustrate some helpful strategic fundamentals. Learning about it now will also help you avoid falling prey to this common trap laid out to catch beginning players.

To achieve Fool's Mate, you must be playing Black. This is somewhat unusual, as White is generally considered to have a very slight advantage over Black on account of making the first move. However, when White opens with the particularly poor start of f3, Black can attempt to initiate this strategy.

Figure 16: In just a single turn, Black has asserted a strong positional advantage over White. From here, a single blunder from White could seal their fate.

Beyond simply leaving White's king open to attack, f3 is a weak opening move because it fails to provide development opportunities for any piece apart from the king itself. Since the king is relatively weak in the opening anyway, this is a major blunder.

33

When Black responds at e5, it demonstrates a strong understanding of opening strategy and positional play. From here, Black's kingside bishop and queen can both take to the field immediately. Opening with a pawn towards the center of the board also allows Black to begin setting up a strong defensive wall in the center of play. Of course, if White makes the mistake of playing g4 next turn, these long-term advantages will cease to matter.

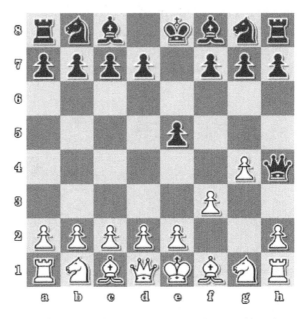

Figure 17: The Fool's Mate has been played to completion. After White moves their pawn to g4 on the second turn, Black responds with a decisive checkmate.

Once again, White has made a blunder on multiple levels. Building a defensive pawn formation on the edges of the board is rarely worth the investment. More importantly, the only piece capable of blocking an attack on the king has given up its ability to do so. Black can easily swoop in with Qh4# to end the game.

While Fool's Mate shows some keen opportunistic play from Black, it's ultimately more of a case study in what not to do from White's perspective. Being caught in this situation can leave a novice player feeling quite embarrassed, but it's simply part of learning the game. Now that you've studied the fastest complete game possible, it's time to examine some deeper chess strategies for different phases of play.

Section 2 – Opening Strategies

The opening ranks begin to mobilize as the pawns start their slow march across the board. Knights take to the field, aiming to thin enemy formations. While bishops begin seeking out the slightest chink in the opposing defense, ready to lash out and escalate the game into an all-out war. The opening game is where strategists begin laying out their elaborate plans, carefully preparing to spring them into action when the time arises.

In technical terms, the opening game is defined as the first few moves of play, where pieces are developed and formations assembled. If that doesn't sound overly specific, it's because it's not. There are no absolute delineations between the phases of a chess game, and often openings and middlegames will overlap.

Chess openings have been studied perhaps more than any other facet of the game, in no small part because many top-level games are won and lost in just the first few moves. Many critical exchanges can take place even in just the first few moves. Even if you're not directly capturing an opponent's piece, shutting down their best-laid plans can establish a positional and mental advantage.

Like any stage of the game, there are boundless ways your opening strategy can take shape. While extreme high-level players study and memorize openings up to dozens of moves, there's no need to be intimidated. While opening strategy is an important aspect of play at any level, it's only one of several stages that make up the full scope of chess strategy.

There are millions of ways a chess game can evolve based on just the first few moves. Still, the most strategically sound openings have been divided into three basic categories: Flank Openings, King's Pawn Openings, and Queen's Pawn Openings. Each of these three categories branches out into dozens of divisions and subdivisions. Still, we'll review just a few of the most popular variations and explore what makes them so effective.

King's Pawn Openings

From turn one, White has 20 possible opening moves, and the King's Pawn Opening of e4 is widely considered as one of the most popular and efficient. This may take new players somewhat by surprise, as it seems to leave the king's file exposed to attack. However, mounting a practical attack on the king remains largely infeasible, especially if White takes advantage of the opportunity to develop both their queen and bishop.

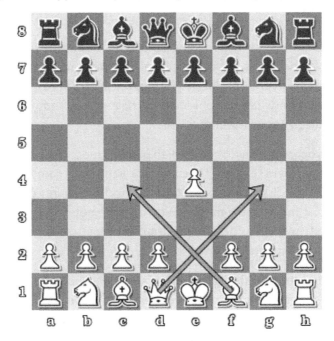

Figure 18: The King's Pawn Opening begins with White's pawn moving to e4. From there, two more powerful pieces can quickly be deployed.

In addition to speeding the development of the queen, e4 is a strong opening because it establishes an early presence at the center of the board. While the downside of this is that White's pawn is temporarily undefended, the player has an opportunity to quickly reinforce it with a robust formation of pawns and harder-hitting pieces.

After such a strong opening, how is Black meant to answer? The most common answer to the King's Pawn Opening is the Sicilian Defense of c5. In fact, this is one of the most common opening exchanges in all of chess. The stark difference in the strategy behind White and Black's opening moves in this scenario perfectly highlights the distinctions of playing as either of the two sides.

Figure 19: In the Sicilian Defense, unlike White, Black's first move to c5 does little to develop pieces. However, there are other substantial advantages.

Whereas White almost always holds an early lead by holding a default initiative, Black must struggle both to halt White's advantage and seize one of their own. Thus, while White's first move in the King's Pawn Opening focuses on asserting quick dominance and pushing a plan into action, the Sicilian Defense is a more reserved response. Black offers White the opportunity to take control of the kingside files quickly, but in exchange, a powerful phalanx of Black's pawns can dominate the queenside field. If Black acts quickly, they can establish their own zone of control while creating a thorny shield against White's attack.

Alternatively, Black may opt for the even more conservative Caro-Kann Defense, in which the pawn moves only one space to c6. This is generally a move favored by more strategic players who seek to establish a long-term positional advantage and are less concerned with opening exchanges.

Of course, some players prefer direct and immediate confrontation. If dynamic play is more of your style, you might answer the King's Pawn Opening with e5, or an Open Game. White will often answer with Nf3, threatening Black's pawn, to which the most common response is Nc6. From there, White attacks the developed knight with Bb5, creating the Ruy Lopez or Spanish Game.

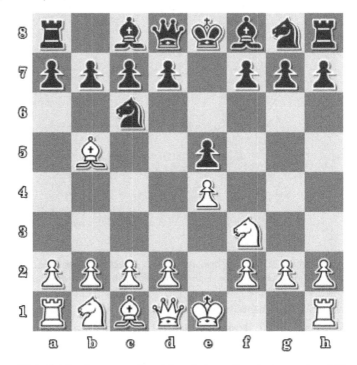

Figure 20: In the Ruy Lopez opening pictured above, threats are made quickly, and both players must leap to action.

One of the fantastic things about the Ruy Lopez is that it offers several viable moves for both sides at almost every point throughout the game. In contrast to more formulaic approaches, Ruy Lopez offers quick-thinking tacticians a veritable buffet line of attacks and gambits to pursue. In fact, there are so many different chains of play that can arise from this opening that it has become one of the most studied phenomena in chess.

While King's Pawn Openings are the most common in high-level play, they're far from the only viable opening strategies. While opening the pawn on the queen's file may not be as popular, it does provide some distinct advantages.

Queen's Pawn Openings

Like the King's Pawn Opening, this opening emphasizes controlling the center of the board from the outset. To begin the game by moving to d4, White prepares to develop the queenside bishop and potentially perform the more difficult queenside castling.

A classic evolution of this opening occurs when black responds with d5, and White proceeds to offer the Queen's Gambit by moving another pawn to c4. Here, Black is faced with a hard decision. They may choose to accept the offered pawn with dxc4, but doing so gives White total control of the center. Alternatively, in denying the bait, Black allows White to pen them in.

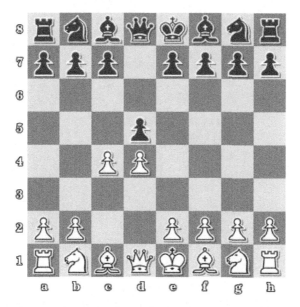

Figure 21: In the Queen's Gambit shown above, White seems to offer Black a pawn, but the gift is poisoned with a difficult choice.

While the Queen's Gambit was extremely popular in the early 20th century, developments in the hypermodern school led to an increasing number of players adopting the Indian Defense and its variations. With this strategy, Black instead opts for the somewhat unusual first-round play of Nf6. Rather than confront White's opening or even attempting to establish their own center of power, Black begins to develop an elaborate web meant to undermine White's supposedly free development.

There are several possible progressions of the Indian Defense, but one of the strongest and most commonly seen in all levels of play is the Nimzo-Indian Defense. In this variation, Black opts to remain flexible for several turns, delaying the building of their own pawn structure with the sole intent of hindering White's.

The standard Nimzo-Indian Defense evolves as such:

1. d4 Nf6
2. c4 e6
3. Nc3 Bb4

Figure 22: In the Nimzo-Indian Defense, Black opts to quickly field their kingside bishop, knowing it will most likely be sacrificed in due time.

40

While both the King and Queen's Pawn Openings derive much of their power from establishing a strong presence in the center, there are always other viable options. The final main category of opening, called the Flank openings, seek to exploit the very concept of central control.

Flank Openings

A reference to military flanking maneuvers, in which one force intercepts the other from the side rather than head-on; the Flank openings avoid the center of the board and threaten from the sides. While any number of different opening moves could be considered a Flank opening, the two most common are 1. Nf3, and 1. c4.

The simplest of the two, 1. c4, is often referred to as the English Opening. In addition to the obvious opportunity to field the queen, this opening also gives White several viable strategies to fall back on, making it difficult for Black to counter. For example, White can easily shift back into a Queen's Gambit or advance into the Réti Opening to threaten from both flanks.

Figure 23: In stark contrast to the King or Queen's pawn openings, the Réti Opening controls the center from outside, rather than within.

41

The Réti Opening is itself normally played as a progression of the Zukertort Opening—the name given to 1. Nf3. Much like the Indian Defenses, which also emphasize the quick deployment of knights, this opening is a strong example of the hypermodern school of strategy. In contrast to classical school, which tends to engage in tactical play, hypermodern players tend to be more fluid strategists. The Réti Opening exemplifies their belief that while the center of the board is an important strategic asset, it is controlled most effectively by outside threats rather than a direct confrontation.

Choosing Your Opening

You've familiarized yourself with the four most popular opening moves: 1. e4, 1. d4, 1. c4, and 1. Nf3. You've also learned ways to advance the game from these openings, whether you're playing on Black or White's side. While various masters have theorized on which of these strategies is the strongest, the truth is that no single sequence of moves will allow you to win every game or even most games. If that were the case, chess would almost certainly lose most of its appeal as a pastime!

Rather than searching for an answer on what the "strongest" opening is, ask yourself instead, what openings are most suited to your style of play? Do you prefer straightforward play rooted firmly in tactical prowess? The King's Pawn Openings may serve you well, while the Queen's Pawn Openings and the Queen's Gambit may be of use to those who enjoy a balance of flexibility and direct confrontation. Or, if you're mostly interested in outmaneuvering and out-scheming your opponents, then the Flank openings may be your most enjoyable path to victory.

You'll also need to consider your opponent if you have enough information to do so. If your opponent has you outmatched in raw tactics, consider a slower-paced opening that will allow you to build out a secured strategy before engaging. On the other hand, you might counter a brilliant strategist with an explosive and direct offensive play that prevents them from setting up their elaborate plans. Above all, always try to keep your opponent guessing and on their toes.

The early exchanges of the opening can produce ripples that are felt throughout the game. However, don't assume that losing your first battle means you've lost the war. Likewise, never assume that your opening strategy was so effective that you could begin to let your guard down. A game of chess can turn over on its head with just a few moves.

Unlike the openings and endgames, the middlegame seems to be the least heavily studied area of chess strategy. However, if one thing is true in chess, it's that no detail can ever be overlooked. As you read on, keep these opening strategies in mind, and consider how they can inform your play as we move into the next major phase of play.

Section 3 – Middlegame Strategies

Opposing forces have clashed, opening blows have been exchanged, and kings have retreated to safety as the battle begins to take shape. We're entering the middlegame, perhaps the most poorly understood of the three segments of play. In technical terms, the opening ends, and the middlegame begins when most or all pieces have been developed, and the king has been maneuvered to a more or less secured location, often through castling.

While scholars throughout the ages have dedicated countless hours to analyze openings and endgame scenarios, the middlegame has received relatively little attention. Partly, this is because the middlegame is so dynamic and difficult to predict. Unlike openings, where only selective moves are available until all pieces have been developed, the middlegame often provides players with a plethora of movement options to choose from. Unlike the endgame, where the number of pieces has decreased, players must account for most of their pieces on the field at once. This can be quite overwhelming for both players and chess scholars alike.

In any case, there are very few proper middlegame maneuvers that can be taught through diagrams. Instead, the middlegame strategy comes down to a set of philosophies and tenets. First, each player must keep their king well-guarded. It's not uncommon for a game to end without reaching the endgame at all if checkmate can be achieved earlier.

Second, players should be seeking out every advantage they can leading into the endgame. This can come in the form of superior positioning or material advantage, preferably both. The middlegame may be a transitional phase of play, but how each player comes out of that transition is sure to have a tremendous impact on the outcome.

In this section, we'll go over the fundamentals of achieving these goals. This section may be more abstract than sections on the opening and endgame, but it's nevertheless an important part of understanding the full scope of chess. Indeed, the logic of opening strategy and the basis of the endgame can only be understood through the lens that divides them.

Positioning the King

Some scholars define the endgame as beginning at a point where the king can effectively take on an offensive role in strategy. Keep this goal in mind as you play, but be wary. The middlegame is a dangerous time for a king. With several enemy pieces active on the field at once, the slightest overextension can leave your most valuable piece open to danger. However, that doesn't mean you can't bolster your king's positional advantage while keeping it thoroughly guarded.

Ideally, by the middlegame, you'll have a sturdy formation of pawns protecting the files near your king, with your major and minor pieces ready to fall back to play defense if the need arises. Castling is one of the best ways to achieve this, as it allows you to keep your pawns on the flank you've castled be in the right formation while those in the center play a more active role on the board.

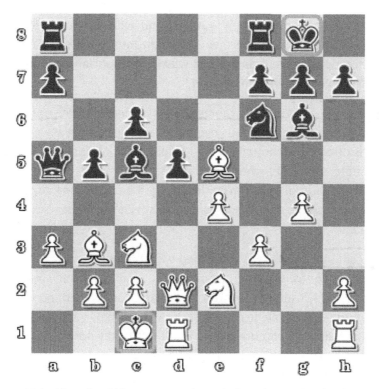

Figure 24: In this early middlegame scenario, each player has castled their king, but otherwise, their strategies are different.

In the figure above, both players have gone to great lengths to secure the king. White has opted for—or been forced into—an extremely defensive formation. While this can provide an effective wall, White runs the risk of being boxed in. Black has taken a more aggressive approach, potentially gaining an advantage if they can maintain the initiative.

Securing Advantages

Assuming your king isn't under threat, the goal of the middlegame is to gain as many endgame advantages as possible. This is done through two primary means, each of which is an intrinsic part of chess strategy: material and board position.

Different masters have differing opinions on which of these is more valuable. Materialists are often more tactical players who value the power and options each piece provides. Positional players tend towards a more detached, strategic outlook, and will sacrifice even valuable material in order to force their opponent into a bad spot. Discovering which type of player you are and why is an important step in finding a comfortable middlegame mindset.

Securing a material advantage means going into the endgame with more *material*—or a higher overall piece value—than your opponent. This is often done through clever gambits, laying traps for the opponent to create scenarios where they're forced to choose which piece to sacrifice. Material gains can be slow to start, but capturing an opponent's queen or rook in the middlegame can speed you to an advantageous endgame.

Positional play is less concerned with targeting individual pieces an opponent controls. Rather, creating an overall favorable spread on the board is this strategy's key to victory. After all, if an opponent's most dangerous pieces can be effectively locked down by your formation, why risk breaking it to capture them? That's not to say positional players are more risk-averse. Many will sacrifice a material advantage for the chance to blow a hole through the enemy's guard.

For beginning players, either option is viable, though both extremes should be avoided. The consequences of all-out materialism or positional play can be offset by some masters, but even then, most strive for a balance that leans towards their preferred method.

In either case, learning to make favorable exchanges is perhaps the most important skill to develop and strengthen your middlegame. In formal terms, an *exchange* refers to the trading of two pieces, but there are positional exchanges to consider as well. Will you abandon your stranglehold on the center of the board to capture an enemy rook? Your answer may well depend on several other factors in the game, and learning to weigh those factors is what makes for great play in the middlegame.

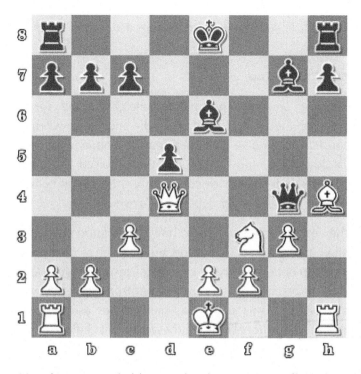

Figure 25: In this scenario, Black has just played Qxg4 and now offers White a hard choice: a potential exchange of queens.

Refer to the diagram above. White can play Qxg4 to capture the enemy queen but will certainly suffer the same fate when Black plays Bxg4. Should White accept Black's offer and exchange queens at this stage?

From a material perspective, White is at a slight advantage, an extra pawn just barely making up the difference for their inferior knight and bishop pair. From a positional standpoint, they also eke out an upper hand over Black, whose pawns are mostly unadvanced and completely unable to protect their exposed king. It would be a gamble, but trading queens here could eliminate a significant wildcard factor from the game and make it easier for White to retain their perilous advantage.

If you're ever unsure whether an exchange is favorable or not, referring back to the valuation system is a good bet. Remember, you usually only want to trade pieces if you're trading a piece of lesser value to capture one of greater value. In some cases, it may be acceptable to trade a knight for a bishop, since bishops are usually more effective in the endgame.

Coming Out on Top

Depending on how the middlegame has gone for you, your perspective on the next phase of play—the endgame—will be drastically different. Players who've outnumbered their opponents secure a solid material advantage, and have a king that's poised and protected can approach this final stage with confidence. Others may not be so lucky. However, the game is never over until it's over.

In the next section, you'll learn how to capitalize on an existing lead to crush your opponents in the endgame as well as how to survive and eke out a comeback victory. If circumstances are truly dire, you'll also learn how to force a draw to save yourself from defeat. As you read on, you can return to this section as many times as needed to review materialistic vs positional play, as these concepts influence every phase of play, despite being most prominent in the middlegame.

Section 4 – Endgame Strategies

The smoke clears across the field of battle, and only a scarce few combatants remain standing on either side. Either both players have executed their middlegame strategies and oppose one another with their favored pieces at the ready, or one player has taken a decisive advantage. It may be a long, brutal hunt before the enemy king is cornered, or it might happen in a single fatal instant. In either case, the endgame is upon them, and only one can win.

As we've already established, phases of play are somewhat malleable, and there's not necessarily a clear indicator of when the endgame begins. In fact, it's not unusual for a king to be checkmated in the middlegame and for the game to close with no endgame at all.

However, a game of chess can be said to have entered its endgame when both players have been reduced to only a few pieces and their kings. Remember, pawns are not considered "pieces" in the technical terms of the game. Often, a pawn's advantage can be the deciding factor in who emerges from the endgame victorious.

In most endgame scenarios, the player who gained a material advantage in the endgame should generally seek to make as many aggressive material trades as possible without sacrificing any pawn. That player's remaining piece(s) can protect pawns on their way to promotion, which is often a death knell for the enemy king. Of course, endgames are extremely varied, and not all of them end with a promoted pawn.

Finally, endgames are characterized by the shift in play where the king becomes a much more powerful offensive tool. Crafty players can weaponize their king to wipe out an opponent's pawn formations or even back the opposing king into a tough spot.

Much like openings, chess endgames are a topic that has been studied extensively throughout the game's history. You can buy dozens of books dedicated to exploring the various endgame scenarios (often called "positions"), many of which feature theoretical exercises that allow students of the game to test their wit and skill. In this guide, we'll focus mainly on the various types of endgames and what beginners need to know to achieve checkmate in each of them.

Endgames Without Pawns

Because of the importance of pawns in the endgame, many players will attempt to eliminate the threat of enemy promotion by wiping their opponent's pawns out entirely. This results in some endgames where there are no remaining pawns at all.

In these scenarios, a king and either a queen or a rook can easily achieve a checkmate against an opponent. Paired bishops on opposite colors also have a fairly simple time achieving checkmate. A bishop and knight will have a much more difficult time, and with two knights, it is nearly impossible to checkmate an opponent, especially if they have a few pieces remaining on the board.

The primary threat in an endgame with no remaining pawns is the possibility of an opponent forcing a draw through a stalemate. Ironically, this becomes somewhat easier for a king pitted against a king and queen, especially if the player with more material is less experienced. Due to the queen's vast range of threatened squares, a wily player can slip their king into position for a stalemate.

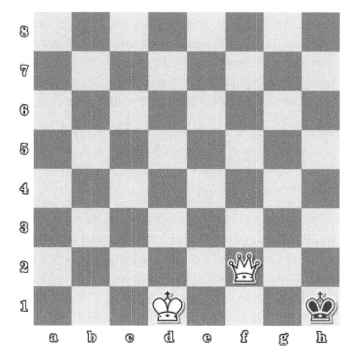

Figure 26: Assuming it's Black's move, this game ends in a stalemate. This is undoubtedly a frustrating prospect for the dominant player.

Fortunately, this type of stalemate is usually easy to avoid once you've become aware of it. Simply remain aware of where your opponent can move on their next turn and ensure there's always at least one safe square available.

Another major factor in endgames with very few pieces, like those discussed here, is the concept of *opposition*. Opposition occurs when two kings are separated from each other only by one rank or file. In this scenario, the player whose turn it is to move has no choice but to move their king away from the enemy, assuming the king is the only piece they can move.

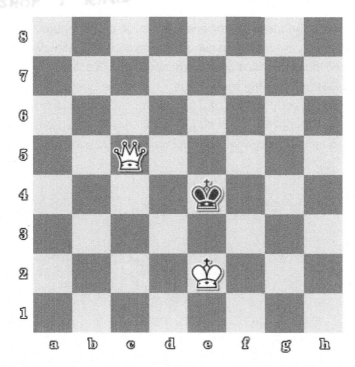

Figure 27: Assuming Black's turn to move, White's king uses opposition to effectively threaten the three squares directly in front of it, cutting off almost half of Black's options for movement and forcing them into an increasingly difficult position.

Opposition can be a decisive factor in nearly every endgame scenario, but it plays an especially critical role in endgames without pawns and — ironically — endgames with only pawns.

King and Pawn Endgames

Sometimes an endgame results in all pieces being captured on both sides, leaving only the kings and their remaining pawns. More than any other endgame, having more pawns than your opponent is key to victory in these scenarios, especially if you have passed pawns on their way to promotion.

In any case, precision is key in a king and pawn endgame, and this becomes truer with the fewer pawns that are remaining on the board. The classic king and pawn vs king endgames have been analyzed endlessly by strategists for this very reason. In such a contest, a single error can turn a win into a draw or a draw into a loss.

51

In a king and pawn vs king endgame, each player's objective becomes clear: the player with the pawn must promote it to achieve checkmate, while the lone king must prevent that outcome in order to secure a draw. To do so, the lone king must either capture the enemy pawn or occupy the square directly in front of that pawn or the square in front of that. By doing so, the lone king can simply cycle through positions to keep the game going indefinitely without the pawn progressing, thereby forcing a draw.

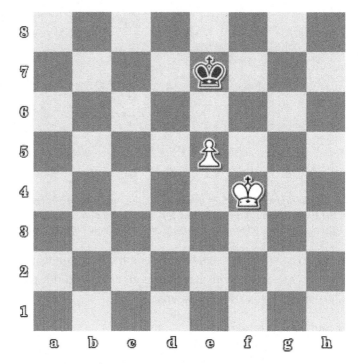

Figure 28: So long as Black plays without error, this game could continue forever. Black has succeeded in forcing a draw.

In these scenarios, where success or failure rides on every single movement, the concept of *triangulation* is essential for both parties. Basically, triangulation in chess refers to the ability of a piece (almost always the king) to return to the same position in three moves. Usually, triangulation also refers to the tactic in which this maneuvering is used to gain a positional advantage over the opponent.

Triangulation can be a tricky concept to grasp in the abstract. To better understand it, let's refer back to the diagram above, but with a few added visual aids.

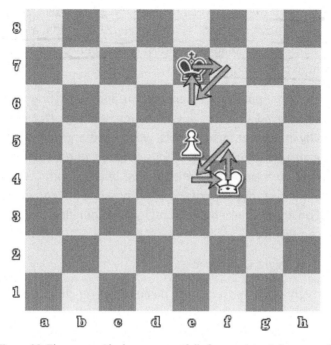

Figure 29: The reason Black can successfully force a draw is because of triangulation.

In this scenario, Black's king must prevent the pawn from progressing, and White's king must remain within one square of the pawn to protect it as it advances. As long as Black continuously cycles through Ke7, Kf7, and Ke6—and always counters White's Kf5 with Kf7—Black will succeed at forcing a draw through the use of triangulation and opposition.

However, if Black isn't properly triangulating, White can also use the same concepts to win. If White can reach a position on Kf5 and Black makes the mistake of responding with Ke7, White will have gained a fatal upper hand. White's pawn can finally advance to e6 while still being protected by its king, and Black will have no choice but to retreat. This is the only scenario in which a long king can still lose when controlling the two squares directly in front of the final pawn in this type of endgame.

In this scenario, Black would likely have preferred not to make a move at all, and simply hold their blocking position indefinitely. However, the rules of chess mandate that each player must move one piece each round. The idea that a player might be forced to move even when it's against their best interests is called *zugzwang*. It's a concept that permeates chess and many other turn-based games, but it's particularly important in chess endgames.

Like that of opposition, triangulation and *zugzwang* are both key concepts to be aware of in any endgame strategy. Not only are they individually important tactical tools, when used together, they also turn your king into an offensive powerhouse capable of turning the tide as the game draws to a close. Now that you've been introduced to all three, you're ready to study some of the other possible endgame scenarios. As you read on, try to think about strategic roles your king could play in each possible endgame.

King and Knight Endgames

The knight is the most difficult piece to deliver checkmate with, since its features are relatively few during endgames, as many players choose to exchange theirs during the middlegame. While a knight can't deliver checkmate on its own, it can work well in tandem with other pieces. Since you can never be sure when you might be forced to enter the endgame leaning heavily on a remaining knight, it's best to understand their endgame strategy, even if it isn't optimal.

Against pawns, a knight's primary objective is to use its jumping ability to weave through enemy blockades and pick off pawns one at a time. A passed pawn can be a nuisance, but the knight should be able to block it, if not capture it before it can promote.

Unfortunately, relying on a knight to stand against rooks, queens, or even bishops often means you're aiming to draw rather than win. The good news is, knights are much more capable defenders in the endgame than they are attackers. By keeping your knight and king close to one another, both pieces can work in tandem to support one another, making it easy enough to draw against stronger piece like a rook.

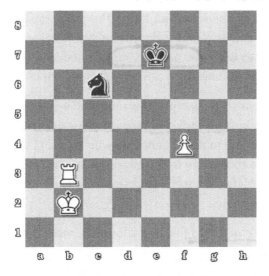

Figure 30: This is a difficult endgame for Black, but not impossible.

In the figure above, Black must stop the advance of the enemy pawn if they're to force a draw. Black's knight will have difficulty capturing the passed pawn, but it can easily block and provide defensive cover while the Black king moves to capture. If the player can pull this off, Black will successfully draw by keeping the king and knight close together and able to protect one another.

With just a few more pieces in play, the knight's defensive capabilities become more of an asset. Even two knights can protect each other and the king well enough to force a draw, if not significantly outnumbered. Still, the knight is generally not a preferred piece to be brought into the endgame and should be sacrificed in favor of a more powerful offensive weapon if possible.

King and Bishop Endgames

While certainly a more versatile attacker in the endgame than a knight, a lone bishop remains incapable of forcing checkmate. With a pair of bishops, this becomes significantly more manageable, since they're both on opposite-colored squares.

One notorious endgame scenario is when each player has only a bishop and pawns remaining, but the bishops are on opposite colors.

Since the bishops cannot attack each other, they must be used primarily as defensive tools to support the players' remaining pawns. This is one of the few cases where a "bad" bishop penned in by surrounding pawns is actually an advantage, as it can provide superior protection.

Bishops are also known for being involved in one of the most common pawnless endgames: a rook and bishop versus one rook. In this scenario, the player with the material generally wins by using the bishop to chase the defender's rook away from squares that allow it to protect its king. With this done, the attacker's rook and king can corner the enemy and achieve a checkmate.

A common counter to this that allows the materially weaker player to draw is the Cochrane Defense. Named from the chess master John Cochrane, the defending player uses the rook to effectively pin the bishop to its king near the center of the board. With only the enemy's rook left as a credible threat, the defender can often force a draw.

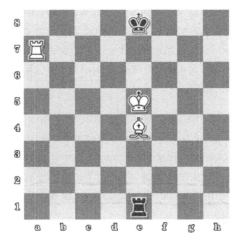

Figure 31: From this position (the Cochrane Defense), Black can endlessly stall out the game with a bit of clever play.

Ultimately, unless they're paired together, bishops are supporters in the endgame, not attackers. As we move on to the more aggressive role of the major pieces in the final game, keep in mind how knights and bishops can be used to support these more powerful pieces if you find yourself with any of these remaining pieces as the game draws to a close.

King and Rook Endgames

Rook endgames are among the most common and best studied of endgames. This is partly because they are always being late to develop and are quite valuable; rooks are not generally exchanged until very late in the game. Another factor is that rook endgames can be extremely complex. On an open board, a rook can generally lock out any rank or file combination in a matter of two moves, often less. This makes pawn promotion much more difficult than in endgames featuring mostly minor pieces.

Especially in a rook and pawn endgame, positioning your rook on the seventh rank can spell doom for your opponent. There are no guarantees, but a rook that controls the seventh rank can sweep up undeveloped pawns while protecting its advancing allies. A famous example comes from the 1924 contest between Jose Raul Capablanca and Savielly Tartakower. In this match, Capablanca successfully infiltrated the enemy lines with his rook leading into the endgame. After a fairly even contest, Tartakower was defenseless against this sudden threat.

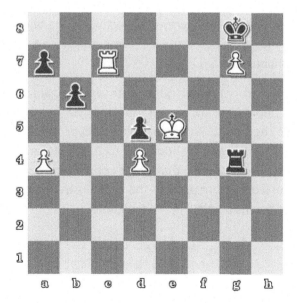

Figure 32: Materially, this endgame may seem dead even, but White's Rook is far better positioned to provide an overwhelming advantage.

Take the diagram above as an example. Assuming Black is to move, they're faced with two equally disastrous options, all thanks to White's rook. They could continue holding back White's pawn with the king, but White's rook will continue to wreak havoc on their pawns. Or, Black could capture the pawn on g7 with their rook, which almost certainly ends with a rook exchange. While Black would end that exchange with one additional pawn, White's king is still far better positioned to support its fewer pawns on their way to promotion. Black almost certainly loses this match.

This is the general principle behind rook endgames—aggression. The rook must seek to wipe out as much enemy material as possible, both to gain a material advantage and increase its mobility.

King and Queen Endgames

Despite its tremendous power, the queen appears in a significantly lower number of endgames than the rook. This may be because queens tend to be more active in the middlegame than the rooks, generally having the side-effect of them being exchanged or otherwise captured before the endgame can begin. Another reason is that due to the queen's ability to overwhelm the enemy while active on the board, many games where the queen is not captured come to an end before a proper endgame can be declared.

If you do hold onto your queen into the endgame, it's a powerful asset. Even on its own, the queen can easily work in tandem with your king to force checkmate. As with a rook, however, the goal of your queen coming into the endgame should be to eliminate any pesky pawn— especially passed pawns—that your opponent still controls. The limitations of a queen are perhaps the best illustration of how important the king and pawns become in the endgame.

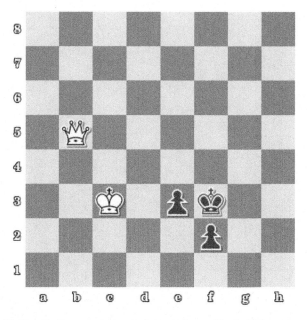

Figure 33: Despite the massive material imbalance, Black still has many paths leading to victory since it already has two passed pawns close to being promoted.

In the figure above, Black has created a strong *fortress*—a formation of pieces that both defend the king and allow the king to defend them. White would have a bout of difficult play ahead even if Black's pawns were still further back, but their position on the second and third ranks makes this situation truly dire. As long as Black keeps a strong formation, White cannot capture without losing their queen, and may as well lose the game. Due to White's poor positioning, Black is likely to be victorious here.

Part of the problem is that in this example, the White king and queen are not positioned to support each other. White's best option is for the king to move to d4 and attempt to capture on e3, but by then, Black will have a promoted pawn defended by its king, and the match becomes materially even.

A far better example of the king and queen working in tandem comes from the 18th-century player François-André Danican Philidor. With both an opening and endgame position named for him, Philidor's contributions to chess analysis are quite weighty.

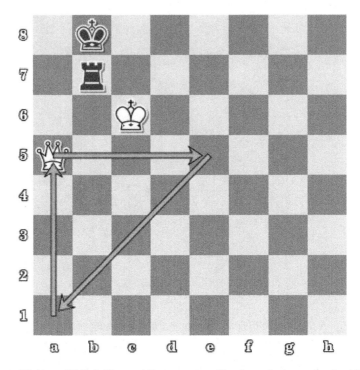

Figure 34: Here, White's King and Queen are working in perfect sync, forcing black into zugzwang *if needed, and securing a victory.*

In this position, analyzed by Philidor, Black is experiencing *zugzwang* if they're to move, their rook forced to abandon its king and weaken both of their positions. If White is to move, they can easily force Black into the same state of *zugzwang* by triangulating with the queen, keeping Black's king in constant check during the process.

Make no mistake—the queen is a fantastic asset in any endgame. However, if there's one thing to learn from this section, it's that positional advantages make more of a difference in the endgame than in any other phase. A poorly positioned queen is easily thwarted by two well-placed pawns, after all.

But what about the human element? We've weighed material factors and positional factors, but if that were all there was to it, chess would be a rather boring game. The truth is, no scenario ever has a truly predestined outcome.

Endgame Theory vs. Reality

Some of the earliest documentation we have on chess analysis has to do with endgame studies. It's a topic that's been analyzed back and forth endlessly over generations of expert players. Today, computer analysis has brought this field of study to new heights, with online databases called tablebases enabling theorists to review exhaustive analysis of endgame positions.

With so much scholarship on the subject, many guides you might refer to will show you a position on the board and state simply that White is sure to win in a certain number of moves. The critical element to remember here is that such declarations assume perfect play on both sides. Two queens *can* certainly outmaneuver a queen in the endgame, but few actual players are also likely to possess the skill to do so too.

Assuming you're playing against others of your skill level, don't be discouraged by high-level theory. These complex scenarios are often meant to illustrate unusual and extreme cases and shouldn't be something you expect to encounter. While master-level players might attempt to reverse-engineer these specific scenarios, for us, they're theoretical illustrations of key concepts that can have a more practical effect on endgame strategy.

By combining your knowledge of key endgame tactics—opposition, triangulation, fortresses, and *zugzwang*, you'll stand a much better chance in an endgame scenario. On top of that, you're now equipped to circle back and apply what you know about all three phases of the game to each other. From setting up in the opening to exchanging in the middlegame, you now possess the tools needed to formulate your own comprehensive chess strategies.

Of course, just like endgame analysis, a study can only ever take you so far. Now that you have the tools, it's time to start putting them into action. In the next section, you'll receive an overview of the various ways you can play the game and start gaining invaluable real-world experience

Chapter 4: How to Start Playing Chess

Congratulations! If you've read this far, you're now a full-fledged student of the game of chess. At this point, you've probably played at least a few games. If you haven't, don't worry. It's never too late to get started, but make no mistake: you must start playing before you can reach your full potential.

Theory and the study of it are important, no doubt. In most scenarios, even a self-taught strategist will have the upper hand over a player relying solely on instinct. At the same time, however, a player with zero practical experience will always be at a disadvantage against an experienced player, regardless of his/her strategy. This is solely because chess, above all, is unpredictable. While theory is useful in outlining the "best" moves from a material and positional standpoint, the human element of chess can never be fully explained by theorists.

In amateur play, opponents rarely stick to by-the-book strategies simply because most players at that level haven't memorized them all. Thus, you can't reliably predict most players move based on theory alone.

This problem only gets worse as you move into professional games. Often, players will attempt to gain a psychological advantage over their opponents by deliberately ignoring or even defying what they know to be the "best" move in a sequence. The psychological elements of chess, the capacity for human error as well as human ingenuity, is something that only experience can fully teach.

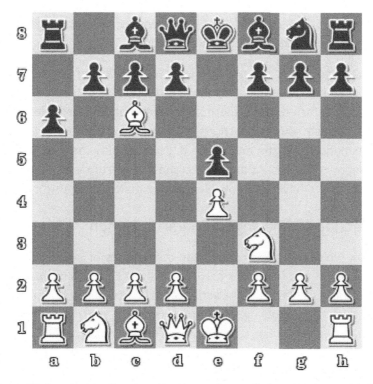

Figure 35: Grandmaster Emmanuel Lasker was frequently known to open with the Ruy Lopez Exchange Variation, widely considered at the time to be poor strategic play. While his defiance of convention certainly gave him a psychological edge over his opponent's, modern strategists now see that Lasker's thinking was ahead of his time.

Don't Get Discouraged

As we've said, you'll be starting at a disadvantage against most experienced players. While this guide can certainly help you narrow that gap, don't worry if you lose your first few games. One of the great things about chess is that even defeat offers opportunities for growth, especially for a trained eye. Very rarely does a match go by without at least one player making a mistake. The ability to spot these errors and learn from them is what makes a great chess player.

But where should you get started? If you have friends or family who are already fans of the game and willing to play with you, you already have a great place to start. However, playing with the same small group over and over will eventually become stale, and may even hinder your technique. This is part of the reason why new, innovative players in the professional scene can be difficult to counter.

When you decide that it's time to step out of your comfort zone and start playing new people, or if you need to look beyond friends and family just to get started, then, there are several options available to you. No matter which route you choose, always remember to practice good sportsmanship. At the end of the day, we all play chess to learn, grow, and enjoy ourselves. As long as you show respect to your fellow players, you're sure to have an enjoyable time, no matter the game's results.

Section 1 – Playing the Game in Person

No, we're not talking about the movements of pieces and opening strategies anymore—From here on forth, it's time for you to get out there and start playing in the active sense! This is one of the most exciting moments in a growing player's career, but also one of the most intimidating. Of course, stepping out of your comfort zone is an essential step along any path to personal growth and learning, but don't feel you have to push yourself too far.

If you're a social person who learns best from talking things out with others, a local chess club may be a good place for you to start. If you'd prefer to learn on your own, at least to start, online chess games might be better suited to your learning style.

In either case, both options come with their share of unique advantages. Ultimately, it's best if you pursue both routes, but choosing where to dip your toe in first can make all the difference.

Joining a Local Chess Club

While somewhat niche, chess is a thriving pastime with players all over the world. Almost every city will have at least one chess club to join, and most are always looking for new members. While most don't advertise heavily, finding a club in your area should be easy with a simple web search. From there, you simply need to do your research.

Some clubs will require formal signup before you arrive at your first event, but in many cases, you can simply show up and start playing.

Generally, it's a good idea to check the club's schedule and see if there are designated meeting times for casual play or even beginner's games. Showing up on your first day to play in a ranked tournament is likely to cause needless stress both for you and the club organizers.

Once you've started with a club, take some time to ensure that it's a good fit for you. Are you having fun playing? Do you feel welcomed into the community? If the scene at one club isn't for you, there's no shame in trying out other groups and locations to see if you can find a better fit. Additionally, while many clubs will allow you to participate for free at first, long-term membership might come with a small fee. It's a good idea to examine all your options before committing to a membership.

Depending on your skill level when you join, you might end up losing more often than not, even against players who are much younger than yourself. Just remember that experience plays a critical role in chess, and one of the biggest benefits of joining a club is the opportunity to learn from these more experienced players. Most of your more skilled opponents will be happy to share pointers. After all, everyone starts from somewhere, and eventually, you'll be the one giving advice!

Playing in Tournaments

Once you've racked up a few wins and gained some valuable experience, you might decide it's time to test your skill in a competitive setting. If going to your first club meeting is an intimidating prospect, your first tournament might cause a degree of anxiety as well. If that's the case, it's a good idea to wait until you feel relatively comfortable, even if you've reached an appropriate skill level. Of course, you can't delay forever and might have to push yourself if you don't feel the confidence arising naturally. For the most part, your club community should be able to provide you with advice on whether you're ready for the big time.

Different tournaments will follow different rules and variations of rules, so it's always good to do your research before attending. Most official tournaments will follow rules standard to a larger chess organization, such as the *Fédération Internationale des Échecs* (FIDE) or United States Chess Federation (USCF). Studying the rules and regulations of such organization can help you to generally prepare for various tournaments under their authority.

By and large, most tournaments are organized according to one of the three basic styles: round-robin, Swiss, and elimination. Each of the three styles comes with its own nuances that contribute to strategy on a game-to-game basis and even a tactical level. Understanding which of the three you're signing up for early on will allow you to strategize around the style's unique qualities.

In round-robin style tournaments, every player faces off against every other player the same number of times. Since everyone faces everyone, many consider this style to be a good judge of pure skill, as it reduces the chance of "unlucky" pairings. However, there are still human elements and elements of chance that contribute to the results of these tournaments. For example, the player's fatigue or mindset can vary from one opponent to the next. A player who suffers an unforeseen loss early on may suffer from a loss of momentum compared to other participants.

Since round-robin tournaments require each player to participate in several matches, it's often used for competitions with a smaller player pool, such as local tournaments or elite championships. The Swiss system, on the other hand, can easily manage hundreds or even thousands of players in a single tournament.

In the Swiss System, players are initially paired off according to their ratings (discussed later in this section). Unrated players are paired off against one another in some other way, such as random or alphabetical assortment. After the first round, winners play against other winners while losers play against losers. This process continues for a set number of rounds until the player with the most wins is declared the winner. In the case of a tie, players may split the prize, or there may be a method of tiebreaking.

The main benefit of the Swiss system, in theory, is that it eventually leads to the most talented players facing one another as they rack up more victories. Unfortunately, some less scrupulous players may attempt to draw a game early on, hoping to face off against weaker opponents while the strongest players duke it out. While this isn't a guaranteed strategy either way, it's certainly frowned upon by most serious players and organizations.

Both the Swiss and round-robin systems generally conform to the same point-scoring method. Usually, a victory is worth one point, a draw is worth half a point, and a loss worth no points (often written out as 1-1/2-0). However, other scoring systems do exist.

In the final type of tournament, however, no scoring system is needed. This is the elimination-style tournament, sometimes called knockout style. In these tournaments, winners progress while losers are simply removed from the competition. Because of this, new and inexperienced players should generally avoid such tournaments, as they'll likely play in fewer games and have fewer chances to learn.

In addition to variations in rules, the timeframe of tournaments may vary widely. Some tournaments space each round of games out for days, while others take place all in the same day. These policies can have a major impact on players' strategies. While long-form tournaments favor careful students who analyze play during their downtime, shorter tournaments can benefit players with greater stamina.

Regardless of the type of tournament you play in, however, you'll have the unique opportunity to participate in post-game analysis. Engaging in analysis with other tournament-level players is one of the best ways to grow as a strategist, in addition to being a rewarding opportunity to meet new friends and potential opponents. Additionally, playing in tournaments allows you to begin building your chess rating.

Your Elo Rating

Once you've participated in a tournament, you'll have the opportunity to earn an Elo rating, which can be improved the more you play in official settings. While some hold the misconception that Elo is an acronym (this is why you'll often see the term capitalized), it actually refers to Arpad Elo, the chess master who created the rating system.

Basically, an Elo rating is a comparative rating designed to calculate a player's relative skill compared with others in their player pool. As a result, different federations have separate Elo rating systems with slight variations on the precise rating method. Because of this, if you were to earn a FIDE rating in your first tournament, you would only be able to build that rating by participating in FIDE-sanctioned competitions.

Additionally, several organizations have different requirements before a rating can be earned. Some organizations require that you score a victory in tournament play before your rating is established, while others supply you with a provisional rating until you've completed a certain number of rated games.

The minimum Elo rating varies depending on the specific implementation of the system in use, but generally speaking, players ranked below 1000 are considered relative novices. Scores up to 2000 are generally considered respectable ratings for developing players, or those who enjoy the game and strategy at an amateur level. At 2000 and above, we start to enter the territory of experts, master, and eventually grandmasters, who must earn a rating in the high 2000s to qualify. The current top-rated chess player, Magnus Carlsen holds a FIDE rating of 2863. FIDE regularly posts updated ratings on their website.

A unique facet of the Elo rating system is that different point values are at stake for either competitor in a rated game. For instance, if a low-rated player and a high-rated player were to end in a draw game, the lower-rated player would improve in their rating, while the higher-rated player's rating would decrease. This is because, rather than being designed as a system of rewarding players for accomplishment, the Elo system uses an impartial statistical method to determine the relative strengths of players.

Section 2 – Playing the Game Online

Maybe you don't feel ready to start meeting up in person and playing chess with strangers. That's understandable. If you haven't had the opportunity to practice with friends or family, starting from zero experience and jumping into live games can be quite intimidating. Maybe your local club's meetings just don't align with your busy schedule, or maybe you're not ready to start paying membership or cost of entry fees yet. If any of these circumstances describe you, playing online is likely your clearest path to getting into chess.

Online chess offers several distinct advantages. For one, you can play as much as you want without ever spending money. You don't even need to buy a chess set! Furthermore, you can play whenever and wherever you want, making it an extremely versatile option for players who travel or have hectic schedules. While it lacks the immediate social engagement and learning opportunities of local play, you'll go on to gain the benefit of playing against a near-endless lineup of opponents from all over the world. This way, you're guaranteed to see countless unique styles and strategies to study and learn from.

While you're trading community for convenience, playing online is a great way to get started as a fledgling player. It's also a solid option for keeping your skills sharp between meetups. As yet another bonus, getting started is as easy as hitting "enter" in your browser's search bar.

Getting Started Online

Most chess sites only require that you have an email address to get signed up. While several sites offer paid subscription models to unlock extra features, you can usually play for free as well, though some sites will restrict how many games or what style of game free users are allowed to participate in.

Before you register, however, you'll need to pick the site that's most suited to your needs. Today's most popular sites are chess.com and chess24, either of which offers excellent free-to-play options as well as advanced training tools for paid members. Another strong option is Lichess, which is equally popular with a somewhat simpler option. Notably, Lichess is completely free and sustained by donations, so while its interface and training tools are somewhat less complex than its competitors, you can access all of them without paying a cent.

Just like different federations, each online chess site ranks players according to its own rating system. So, no matter how high your rank is on chess.com, you'll be starting from scratch on a different site or in a live tournament. Unlike live tournaments, however, getting your starting rating is usually much simpler. As soon as you start playing, you'll begin building your rating. You may lose your first set of games, especially if you're coming to the site without any experience, but eventually, you'll settle into a tier with other players of your skill level. From there, it's just a matter of training until you can move up to a higher rating and hold onto it.

Types of Games

Unlike in-person games of chess, where two players sit down across a table from one another, there's no way to be sure what your opponent is up to on the other side of your computer screen. Due to this, online chess matches have had to find some method of ensuring that players don't simply walk away from a game whenever they please. Or, if they do abandon a match, those players ought to face repercussions.

This has resulted in two types of chess becoming most popular for online play: blitz chess and correspondence chess. The former option ensures that players who leave a game are given a loss, while the latter embraces the option for players to take their time between each move. After all, that digital board isn't going anywhere.

Blitz chess games can be of variable length, but they're defined by using time-control of no longer than 10 minutes. That is, each player has their own clock with ten minutes or less on it, which starts counting down at the start of each of players turns and stops when that player's turn is over. If you take one minute to make each of your moves, you'll have only ten moves in which to win. If your clock runs out, it's game over, and you lose even if you had a clear advantage. This can be frustrating at first, but it introduces a new layer of strategy to the game: can you keep your cool and make the right moves, even when your clock is ticking down?

In fact, most competitive chess games utilize some form of a time limit, though usually, it is much more forgiving. It's not uncommon for chess games to take up to two hours in tournament settings. However, in a blitz game, there's a 20-minute maximum. This drastic difference means that blitz chess can help you sharpen your quick-thinking abilities compared to the traditional play, but you may miss out on some of the more deep-thinking elements of strategy.

For an extreme example of deep-thinking chess and a chance to hone your long-form skills, there's correspondence chess. Originally, this was a form of a long-distance game in which opponents would send each other moves by letter, hence the name. With the advent of the internet, correspondence chess has moved on to email and even designated correspondence servers.

Perhaps the extreme opposite to blitz games, correspondence chess can take days, months, or even years just to complete a single game. Due to its slow-paced nature, it's not only an excellent exercise in deep, methodical play but a chance to form long-lasting connections with fellow chess enthusiasts. After a month-long correspondence game with someone, taking days or weeks at a time to assess their strategy, you'll have made a bond for life.

Where to Jump in

There's no single correct way to start playing chess, but hopefully, by now, you should have a clearer idea of how you'd prefer to proceed. While chess clubs offer deep social experiences and learning opportunities, online chess can be a more convenient and less intimidating option.

For most players, getting some practical experiences at home or online can help prepare you for club-level play. If you're confident in your skills or don't mind taking a few losses, there's nothing wrong with jumping straight into your local club scene. Ultimately, serious players will eventually want to join a club, as it connects them with the local community and helps keep them up to date on upcoming tournaments. However, you can still develop a rich knowledge and enjoyment of chess simply by playing online or with your friends at home.

In any case, by simply playing the game, you can always be in the most reliable path to fun and improvement. As you gain experience, you may begin to seek out ways to supplement your natural progression. Fortunately, for dedicated students, there are always more opportunities to learn.

Section 3 – The Road to Mastery

At this stage, you've hopefully had the chance to gain some practical experience with the game. Even if you haven't, don't worry. You'll play your first game eventually! Once you've mastered the basic flow of the game and started developing your own strategies, it's time to take it to the next level. There are several avenues to further supplement your understanding, both through formal training and independent study.

While this book has provided you with all the basic knowledge you need to understand the mechanics and strategies of chess, along with how to start playing yourself, it's also a guide designed for beginners. Soon, that won't be you. When that day comes, this section can help you find an entry point for further development as an intermediate or advanced player.

As with anything in the game of chess, different types of players will benefit more from different approaches. Some might prefer the direct approach of a chess tutor, while others will learn best from seeking out their answers. In the end, the path is yours to shape as you see fit. After all, if there's one thing you've learned by now, it's that chess is a near-infinitely deep game with the potential to provide a lifetime of new lessons. So long as you continue to seek out knowledge, you're sure to find more of it.

Finding a Teacher

Naturally, one of the most tried and true methods of gaining knowledge in any subject is to learn from someone with more experience. Taking lessons from a professional chess instructor is a great way to learn from them directly, as well as give yourself a skilled opponent against whom you can test new strategies. Just like chess clubs, finding an instructor in your area is easily done with a simple web search. In fact, many clubs offer training programs or can put you in contact with individual instructors.

Of course, there's no need to rush learning from the first instructor you find. In addition to offering different rates and lesson plans, every instructor will have a differing teaching style that may or may not blend well with your needs and expectations. Be sure to shop around—there's no shortage of able teachers out there. Meanwhile, many acclaimed instructors now offer lessons over the internet, putting you in touch with plenty of great options.

In addition to direct lessons, many chess experts have created intermediate and advanced level books, videos, and computer programs to help rising talent reach their goals. All the chess websites mentioned earlier in this chapter offer either free or paid training tools for users. In conjunction with professional instruction or even on their own, these programs offer a great path to enhancing your skills as a player. For self-motivated students who prefer to work at their own pace, those might even be the best option available.

Of course, there may eventually come a time where you would have learned everything a book, program, or even an instructor can teach you. When that time arrives, don't worry. There are still more steppingstones ahead.

Studying the Masters

So far, this book has touched very little on many of the theories espoused by the hundreds of masters and grandmasters who have helped the game evolve over the years. In large part, that's because many of these ideas are beyond the scope of a beginner's guide. Not only do they assume a complex and nuanced understanding of chess theory, but many of the topics are also so elaborate that they require their own books to adequately explain them!

To some, this is an intimidating prospect. What it means in practical terms is that there's a treasure trove of expert-level knowledge out there, simply waiting for you to take it in. If at first some of the materials suggested in this section ends up being too complex, don't worry. You can and should return to it later. Most of the material referenced is aimed at players in the 1000-plus ratings who are seeking for master or grandmaster candidacy.

As an entry point, titles like Jeremy Silman's *How to Reassess Your Chess* can be extremely handy. While exploring the highly complex positional theory, Silman's greatest strength is perhaps in introducing information in a way that is relatively unintimidating compared with other authors. Regarding this, even players in the mid or lower 1000 ratings can gain significant rewards from his teachings.

Other examples that may be more appropriate for intermediate, as well as advanced readers, are more biographical or autobiographical works. Since these books can be read almost like a story, it provides more concrete detail for the reader to latch onto, making it far easier to understand the complex theory that's at the heart of the writing. Bobby Fischer's *My 60 Most Interesting Games* is perhaps one of the best-known examples of such a title, though lesser-known gems such as *The Life and Games of Mikhail Tal* also provide exquisite strategic knowledge.

Then, of course, there are the classics. Aron Nimzowitsch's *My System* was originally published in the early 20th century during the advent of hypermodern thinking in the chess world. Despite being nearly 100 years old, it's still considered an integral part of the chess player's canon today, and one of the most influential books ever published on chess strategy. In fact, many of the core tenets of positional play discussed in this book were originally outlined in Nimzowitch's writings.

You may also find out that, as you develop as a player and strategist, you would like to fill out holes in your ability or further sharpen your strengths. There are many intermediate and expert-level books on highly specialized topics. Ladimir Vukovic's *The Art of Attack in Chess*, for example, focuses exclusively on the many ways in which to attack the opponent's king. Both Dvoretsky's *Endgame Manual* and Shereshevsky's *Endgame Strategy* deal specifically with the final phase of the game, and both are highly regarded within the chess community.

As you may have guessed, many of these titles were originally published in languages other than English, so you may need to look carefully to ensure the publisher's translation accurately captures the nuance of the author's original language.

Chess Databases

Finally, you'll discover that independent analysis of real chess games offers deep insight for players to grow from. Beyond analyzing your own chess games, studying the actual moves played by masters and grandmasters can help you grow to better understand their mindsets and strategies. While this used to be a difficult thing to study, today's chess databases provide play-by-play synopsis of millions of chess games played at various skill levels up to grandmaster.

Among the best-known chess databases is chess-db.com, which offers full reviews of nearly 10 million games: You'll as well find a similar database on chesstempo.com. Beyond allowing you to replay each move of a game, both sites and other similar ones offer additional tools and data as well. For example, data on which moves increase a given color's chances of victory at any point in a match can be quite useful, provided they're reviewed with proper understanding and not simply taken for granted.

Some sites and apps even use their data to create programs specifically designed to mimic the chess strategy of famous players. While it's certainly not the same thing as playing a grandmaster, these programs can be an entertaining way to study both your own and others' styles of play.

Never Stop Playing

It's a long road ahead, but the basic tenets of improving as a chess player are the same as in any other endeavor: To get better, you must practice. That means playing whenever you can, even if it's only a game a day, a game a week, even a game a month. You may see results faster by playing more, but no matter how much time you dedicate, you're sure to improve if only you can stick to it.

There may be times when you feel frustrated, or like your skill has reached a plateau you can't surpass. Certainly, everyone who's ever played has felt that way at some point or another. This is where the real battle is. You may feel you've reached a higher level of play at one moment only to feel you've hit a wall of more skilled players in the next.

The simple beauty of chess is that on any given day, in any given game, either player has a chance of winning. There will be days when the odds, your luck, possibly even your mindsets out to defeat you. Every player has had that experience.

Keep playing. Just as there are moments of doubt and frustration, chess offers countless unique opportunities to experience uplifting joy and excitement. Whether it's a come from behind win, finally defeating a mentor, or the simple joy of spending time with friends, what makes chess truly special is more than just mechanical depth—it's the appreciation for that depth and the boundless opportunities to explore it.

Now that you've completed this guide, you've already taken your first big leap into your own personal relationship to the game. Chess rewards mastery, but the game itself doesn't distinguish between hobbyists and elites. Anyone, no matter how skilled, can have a deep personal connection to chess. No matter what yours is, we wish you luck in pursuing it far into the future.

Glossary of Terms

Chess is an ancient game, with dozens of variations and hundreds of terms emerging from its extensive history. While the entire book has been dedicated entirely to chess terminology, this glossary provides definitions for all the terms referenced in this guide.

Attack

Any action on the board aimed at capturing or threatening an opponent's piece is considered an *attack*. This can be as simple as overrunning an enemy bishop with your rook, or as complex as maneuvering a knight with the intent of forcing your opponent to make an error.

Capture

A piece that moves into a space occupied by a piece of the opposite color has *captured* the opposing piece. The opposing piece is removed from the board, and the piece that moved into its space now occupies that square. Capturing an opponent's pieces is one of the most common methods of gaining an advantage.

Check

When an attack directly threatens a king's square, that king is said to be *in check*. The player whose king is threatened must ensure the king's safety either by moving the king or by blocking the king's square with a piece, or you end up losing the game. Though it is customary to declare "check" aloud when you've threatened your opponent's king, there's no formal rule requiring you to do so.

Checkmate

Checkmate occurs whenever a king is directly threatened, and no legal move would allow that king to escape. When a player's king is checkmated, that player loses the game.

Connected Pawns

We say pawns are *connected* when two or more pawns of the same color are on adjacent files. Connected pawns are able to support each other and are considered stronger than isolated pawns.

Defense

When either player moves in response to the attack of their opponent, that player is utilizing *defense*. A clumsy defense might open the player up to further attacks, but a well-considered counterattack can allow a defending player to retake the initiative.

Development

One of the most critical aspects of an opening strategy is the *development* of major and minor pieces by moving them from their original spaces on the board. A developed piece can take a more active role in the game.

Figurine

A *figurine* can refer to a physical playing piece in chess. In chess notation, it also refers to the symbols representing those pieces. For example, a figurine of a white king is presented here: ♔

File

The vertical columns on a chessboard are called *files*. In algebraic notation, files are numbered a-h, starting from White's left-hand side of the board.

Fortress

An important concept in the endgame, a *fortress,* is any formation of pawns and pieces that forms a barrier around the king. This is a powerful warding tactic, as it keeps the king safe while also allowing it to strike back against anything that threatens its defenders.

Initiative

Whenever a player is attacking and forcing their opponent to respond, that player is said to have the *initiative*. In almost every case, the defending player must take the initiative if they are to win the game.

Major Piece

The *major pieces* are the queen and rooks. Major pieces are considered more valuable than their minor counterparts because they have increased mobility and range, making them capable of checkmating an enemy king relying only on their own king for support.

Match

Not to be confused with a game, a chess *match* is any competition between individuals or teams that takes two or more chess games to decide. Competitive play often involves matches that span several individual games.

Material

Every piece on the board is considered *material*. Having more material value on the board than your opponent provides a significant advantage, but it doesn't ensure your victory.

Minor Piece

Knights and bishops are considered to be *minor pieces*. Their restricted mobility prevents them from checkmating an enemy king on their own, but this doesn't mean these pieces are weak. The effective use of minor pieces is an integral part of a chess strategy.

Notation

Notation is the means by which chess moves are recorded. The most commonly used and understood form of notation today is the algebraic notation. This book uses algebraic notation alongside diagrams.

Opposition

Opposition describes the phenomenon in which two kings are positioned no more two squares away from one another. The king with initiative forces the enemy king to move away, as the king cannot draw closer without putting itself in check.

Passed Pawn

A pawn without any opposing pawn ahead of it on the same or adjacent files is called a *passed pawn*. They're considered valuable because they stand a better chance of being promoted.

Position

In chess theory, a *position* is any arrangement of pieces on the board. It also carries the colloquial meaning. You might refer to a piece's position on the board or the position of the entire board.

Rank

Each horizontal row on a chessboard is called a *rank*. In algebraic notation, the ranks are numbered 1-8, starting from White's side of the board.

Strategy

Strategy involves long-term planning and decision making. A player's strategy consists of their goals throughout an entire game, or often several games in a match. While strategy is generally the basis for a player's tactics, this is not always the case.

Tactics

A player's *tactics* are the moment-to-moment movements that they employ to gain an immediate advantage over an opponent. Examples of tactics include springing a trap on your opponent or sacrificing a piece. Tactics are often informed by strategy but may change drastically even in a single game.

How to install a magnifying glass

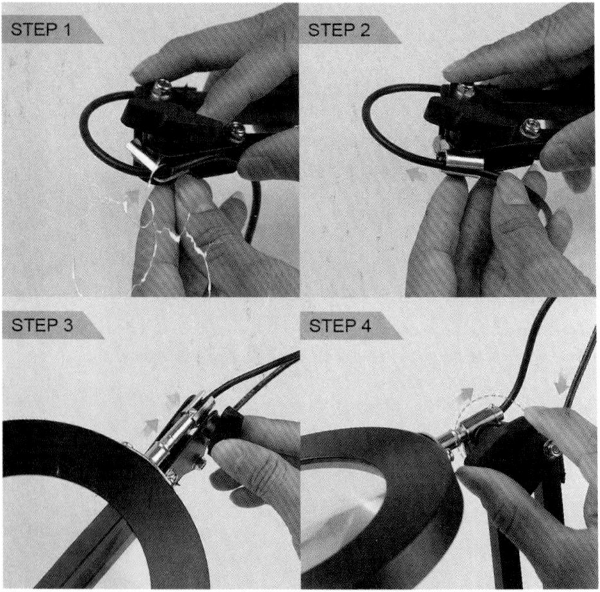

STEP 1

STEP 2

STEP 3

STEP 4

1. After you get the product, staggered the metal piece, put the wire into the metal sheet .

2. Adjust the metal piece and wire , let the USB control wire passes freely in the middle

3. Slowly twist the button ,let the screws hold the metal piece and the usb wire

4. Twist this to the tightest, you will get a connected device with a USB controller and a magnifying glass

Here is two clamp ways : Horizontal Clamp or Vertical Clamp

How to clamp your lamp on the desk?

Please follow this step to install the clamp.

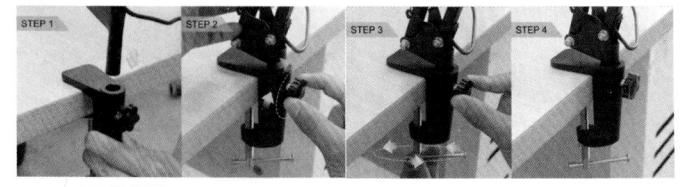

STEP 1　STEP 2　STEP 3　STEP 4

ecification:

.D: 72 SMD Led light

harge : 5V 2A

agnifying Glass Multiple: 5X LED Magnifying Glass

aterial: Aluminum alloy + metal + K9 optical glass

ackage including:

pcs Aluminum Alloy Base

pcs Magnifying Glass

pcs Mini Spanner

You can use it as a daylight bright desk lamp that gives you enough soft light when reading a book, provide Cool / Warm Illumination so you can see details clearly and colors accurately.

Usage Method:

1. Please follow the Structure diagram to set up the whole product.

2. Plug in the USB cable into any DC-5V power source, such as a cellphone wall adapter, laptop or power bank.

3. Once plugged in, long-press the power on the USB cable to turn the LED lights on.

4. You can change the light color or adjust the brightness in the control switch.

Warnings:

1. Do not place the magnifying glass in direct sunlight. Reflection of direct sunlight by the glass could cause a fire.

2. Wipe the lens with the included cleaning cloth to prevent scratching.

3. Never use detergent, gasoline, furniture polish, paint thinner, o other chemicals to clean any part of the magnifying glass, as it will damage the lens.

4. The unit is not waterproof and should never be used in wet conditions.

How to install a magnifying glass lamp:

For transportation safety and convenient packaging, we loosened the magnifying glass for this product. The wire can be twitched to adjust the length for easier to install magnifying glass lamp with holder.

Make sure the fixed knob is tightened before using the lamp.

<u>Triangulation</u>

A piece is *triangulating* when it returns to the same position in the course of three moves. This is usually done by a king with the intent of gaining a positional or initiative advantage over the enemy.

Zugzwang

Literally translated from German as "compulsion to move," *zugzwang* is a condition in which a player would be strategically better off if they took no moves on their turn but must move a piece to comply with the rules of the game.

"How To Reassess Your Class"
by Jeremy Silman

"My 60 Most Interesting Games"
by Bobby Fischer

"My System"
by Aron Nimzowitsch } early 1900s
(twentieth century)

"The Life and Games of Mikhail Tal"
by Mikhail Tal

4/18

Vermell

8/10 — Thursday   8:10 AM

048/08   8:10

@ Ely

Made in the USA
Monee, IL
25 February 2021

61343784R00049